The Thorn of a Rose
Amy Lowell Reconsidered

The Thorn of a Rose

Amy Lowell Reconsidered

BY
GLENN RICHARD RUIHLEY

ARCHON BOOKS
1975

Library of Congress Cataloging in Publication Data

Ruihley, Glenn Richard.
    The thorn of a rose: Amy Lowell reconsidered.

    Bibliography: p.
    1. Lowell, Amy, 1874-1925. I. Title.
PS3523.088Z75   811'.5'2 [B]   74-13542
ISBN 0-208-01458-6

© 1975 by Glenn Richard Ruihley
First published 1975 as an Archon Book,
an imprint of The Shoe String Press, Inc.,
Hamden, Connecticut 06514

PRINTED IN THE UNITED STATES OF AMERICA

For Humberto
and Paula Ruihley Urrutia

On this wondrous sea,
   Sailing silently!
   Ho! pilot, ho!
Knowest thou the shore
Where no breakers roar,
   Where the storm is O'er?

In the silent west
Many sails at rest,
   Their anchors fast;
Thither I pilot thee,—
Land, ho! Eternity!
   Ashore at last!

EMILY DICKINSON

Contents

Preface

Shall I uncrumple this muchly crumpled
thing?   WALLACE STEVENS

When Amy Lowell died in 1925, in mid-career and at the height of her powers, she was regarded by most literate persons as the foremost American poet. Her eminence was not due solely to the appeal of a picturesque and unique personality. It was based, first of all, on some of the most original and expressive poems to be found in recent American literature.

The poems concerned were expressive of a distinctive mode of thought with a novel perspective and approach to meaning. The approach was impressionistic, that which the mind can discover through direct observation and its powers of intuition. The perspective was novel in that it focused on objects in the immediate foreground of life: flowers, trees, sky, or a lightly sketched nude, "slim and without sandals"; and then, in the far distance, the faint outlinings of a limitless spiritual realm which was their source and meaning. What this perspective minimized was the "quotidian," the exigent middle ground of existence, the ordinary daily concerns in which most human lives are entirely absorbed. From the vantage point of her aristocratic grandeur, the solitude of her celibate life, and the demands of a probing intellect no other approach and perspective were possible. Without conscious choice or direction, Miss Lowell's nature and circumstances guided her along this path, away from ordinary routines of existence in favor of explorations of what Wallace Stevens has called "the indefinite, the impersonal, atmospheres and oceans and, above all, the principle of order."

The perusal of Amy Lowell's poetry has always shown that she was, in fact, preoccupied with "atmospheres and

oceans." It is the principal complaint against her that she
was chiefly attracted to the "shining shells" of things, that
her real successes were in the depiction of the external
world and that she failed to do justice to the emotions and
inner experience of man. This is true in the sense I have
suggested above. But it is not true to say that Miss Lowell's
poems are skillful color photographs which leave the
vital issues of life untouched. Detached from the middle
distances in which we realize ourselves in exaggerated self-
importance, Amy Lowell's penetrating gaze sought and
found, not flowers and trees or spare-limbed nude, but
the spiritual presences that these forms manifest to the
sensitive eye and ear.

The "unseen faces of the gods" as the true object of the
poet's quest is the theme of the verses by de Regnier that
Miss Lowell chose as motto for *Sword Blades and Poppy
Seed,* her first volume in the Imagistic manner. In this way
she connects the two major stages of her work: the early
poems, collected in *A Dome of Many-Coloured Glass,* which
are mystical in subject matter and the poems of her artistic
maturity in which her apprehensions are presented in-
directly by means of visual images. Eschewing traditional
bodies of religious belief or philosophic thought, Miss
Lowell responded to her world impressionistically and so
gave varied testimony to the Divinity she felt but could not
either name or categorize.

That her need for exploration was great is proved by the
vast bulk of her output. In the years between 1914 and 1922,
when Wallace Stevens was accumulating the seventy-six
poems that appeared in his first volume, Miss Lowell wrote
eight thick books of verse (one of them still unpublished)
totaling 322 poems. Many of these poems consisted of two
or three lines, but others were of epic length and pre-
tensions and they included work in nearly every variety of
poetic expression, some of them very ill-suited to Miss
Lowell's gifts. As one would expect, the quality of this
work was as uneven as its quantity was great. Some of her
narrative poems sink into arid verbalism. A large part of her

published work consists of technical exercises, preparatory sketches for other poems, or descriptive matter without a true core of thought or feeling. Unrewarding as such poems may be, they were the necessary preliminaries to her moments of genuine inspiration and these were frequent enough to produce a large body of distinguished work. In the words of John Lowes, written shortly after the poet's death, "She has added new beauty to English poetry. How great that contribution is will first be clearly seen when time has winnowed and her enduring work is brought together in one rare and shining book."

The views of Professor Lowes expressed the judgment of most serious readers in 1925, and they are a reasonable statement of Amy Lowell's rightful place in American literature. But the winnowing process of which he speaks has never taken place. Even before 1925 a new and stringent orthodoxy governing the form and content of poetry had begun to establish itself under the leadership of T. S. Eliot and Ezra Pound. A spirit as free and generous as that of Miss Lowell (and a poetic performance so halting) could never satisfy the narrow, dogmatic, and reactionary conceptions of these two men. As the followers of Eliot and Pound, the so-called "new critics," gained decisive control over literary opinion beginning in the 1930s, Miss Lowell was first ignored and then universally denigrated. Today she is excluded from all anthologies representing fashionable taste so that her work is virtually unknown to younger readers. This is our loss, for few poets offer so dazzling an image of our world, both in the poems she wrote and in the qualities we find in her life.

In this work I have endeavored to redress the balance of opinion in Miss Lowell's favor. To do so it is necessary to understand the inner character of her life and work apart from the glittering surfaces of both. In the first chapter I describe the principal elements of Amy Lowell's life: the inner psychic conflict and human traits that shaped her work, including her anomalous position as rebel-aristocrat. The chapter takes the form of disconnected vignettes because I have sought to focus and crystallize some of the strangeness, drama, or beauty which I found in the poet's real life. In the conclusion to this chapter the nine sections are completed by a continuous narrative of the poet's life beginning with family origins and birth to the publication of her first volume of poems at the age of thirty-eight. Chapters two, four and five describe her life and work in three successive periods: early, middle, and late. Chapter three is an effort to provide a philosophic framework for Miss Lowell's poetry by describing the Zen Buddhist contribution to the formation of Imagist poetry, including her own. With a few notable exceptions Imagist verse has always been treated as realistic sense impressions. I believe that this is to miss the real nature of the poetry and it is hopelessly inadequate as an explanation of the mesmerizing power of Amy Lowell's best work. Miss Lowell's mind was deeply colored by her life-long interest in the Orient as it was by her interest in European Impressionism, and these were two currents which fused in her consciousness to produce the masterful art of her middle and late periods. The purpose of this study is to foster appreciation of that art by analysis of its novel qualities and the meanings it contains.

G. R. R.

Acknowledgments

Having begun the research for this study many years ago, I was fortunate in obtaining the reminiscences and views of a number of persons closely connected with Amy Lowell. These included Lorna Russell Amussen, the daughter of Amy's companion; Katherine Putnam Bundy, the poet's niece; Dr. Millicent Todd Bingham; Jean Starr Untermeyer and John Farrar, who were literary associates; S. Foster Damon, Miss Lowell's biographer; and especially Barbara Higginson Wendel, close friend and companion of Miss Lowell's youth. All of these persons provided valuable glimpses into Amy's life as did Mr. and Mrs. Thomas M. Claflin, who showed me the rooms of her home now owned by them and provided me with information concerning the character of the estate during the poet's lifetime.

In writing the doctoral dissertation from which this book is derived I had the assistance of Professor Herbert F. Smith who counseled me regarding its content and style. During my visits to Cambridge and Chicago to read the private papers of Miss Lowell, I had the courteous cooperation of the staffs of the Houghton Library at Harvard and the Harriet Monroe Collection at the University of Chicago. In another direction, that of defining the philosophical significance of Amy Lowell's poems, I am indebted to Leonard Otto, who brought to light hidden links between her insights and systems of developed thought such as Zen Buddhism. Professor Joe Lee Davis read the manuscript in its original form and offered invaluable suggestions and encouragement.

I also wish to express my gratitude to various friends whose interest fortified me in carrying out my tasks. Among these were Professor Henry F. Wells, Margaret Carpenter, Professor Peter Van Egmond, Joseph Buresh, John Beutel, Vera Meyer, Elaine Canfield Ruihley, Sarell Beal and Charles W. Goan. My two typists, Vernal Solveig in Madison and Norma Feldkamp in Ann Arbor, performed indispensable services as well. Lastly, I wish to record my gratitude to my parents, Mr. and Mrs. E. Forest Ruihley, who provided a large part of the funds needed for my livelihood during the time I was writing this study.

The poetry of Amy Lowell is used by courtesy of the Houghton Mifflin Company, Boston; the poetry of H. D. by courtesy of Grove Press, New York.

Chapter One

The Empress of Brookline

I

A Fairy Tale

In a diary that survives from her sixteenth year, Amy Lowell remarks that she would "like to write—as if somebody were going to read this." The idea is interesting in view of the contents of this journal. More than usually intimate, it is the forthright statement of the full complexities of her emotional life. Nothing is lacking. Even the language has the succinctness and immediacy characterizing her later verse. The emotional dilemmas which are her theme are viewed honestly and there is no self-pity, although there is also no hope.[1] In the thirty odd years remaining in her life, nothing was to disprove these girlhood insights. The emotions of the poet continued to be intractable, and Miss Lowell remained alone, cut off from the fulfillments which were essential to her well-being.

Something of her circumstances and this painful state of mind are expressed in her poem, "The Fruit-Garden Path":

> The path runs straight between the flowering rows,
> A moonlit path, hemmed in by beds of bloom,
> Where phlox and marigold dispute for room
> With tall, red dahlias and the briar rose.
> 'Tis reckless prodigality which throws
> Into the night these wafts of rich perfume
> Which sweep across the garden like a plume.
> Over the trees a single bright star glows.
> Dear garden of my childhood, here my years
> Have run away like little grains of sand;
> The moments of my life, its hopes and fears
> Have all found utterance here, where now I stand;
> My eyes ache with the weight of unshed tears.
> You are my home, do you not understand?[2]

The poem is notably reticent but its aim is not self-expression, as in the diary, but the exposure of the major tension in her life. In this connection, one notes that the sonnet is entitled "The Fruit-Garden Path," and in the last line the poet refers to this place as her home. That we are meant to take this seriously is emphasized by the fact that this magnificent garden, bordering the fruit trees on the Lowell estate, is the refuge where she has bared her innermost life. But there is a bizarre disconnection between the two images she has juxtaposed here. If the garden is her home and emblem, it is because she is at one with its dazzling and fructifying life. But this splendor, so vividly conceived, has to do only with the frame of Miss Lowell's life. In the sestet of the poem, we are back once more in the world of the diary: the image which completes the brilliance of the garden is that of a sterile and blighted life. Nor is this overstatement. Amy Lowell never recovered from the emotional denials of her youth, and the conflicts this produced became the essence of her inner history.

The emotions involved are well expressed in the unsparing language of "A Fairy Tale," another early poem. In a gentle revery the poet relives the story of the princess born into an enchanted castle but cursed by "an unbiden guest" on the day of her christening. In the concluding passage the tone intensifies as the poet applies the story to herself.

> The fire falls asunder, all is changed.
> I am no more a child, and what I see
> Is not a fairy tale, but life, my life.
> The gifts are there, the many pleasant things:
> Health, wealth, long-settled friendships with a name
> Which honors all who bear it, and the power
> Of making words obedient. This is much;
> But overshadowing all is still the curse
> That never shall I be fulfilled by love!
> Along the parching highroad of the world
> No other soul shall bear mine company.
> Always shall I be teased with semblances,
> With cruel impostures, which I trust awhile

Then dash to pieces, as a careless boy
Flings a kaleidoscope, which shattering
Strews all the ground about with coloured sherds.
So I behold my visions on the ground
No longer radiant, an ignoble heap
Of broken, dusty glass. And so, unlit,
Even by hope or faith, my dragging steps
Force me forever through the passing days.

[*CP*, 12-13]

In the setting of scholarly analysis, the poem may seem melodramatic, but it is not so in the context of Miss Lowell's life. The experience of literary success would modify her self-image, but the core of unfilfillment remained. It furnishes the principal theme of her lyrical and narrative verse as well as the edge of tragic awareness which energizes her poetry as a whole.

II.

The Thorn of a Rose

Portrait photography is remarkable sometimes for its reticence, and Amy Lowell had more reason than most to wish to "edit" her likenesses. However, we have at least one photograph of her of an unsparing realism. It is a snapshot of Miss Lowell at the Hotel Astor, seated with other persons after a poets' banquet. Fastidiously and even lavishly arrayed, she is ill-served by the very richness of her costumes.[3] What we see in fact is an insane profusion of flesh, and this photo, later printed in a newspaper, might well have inspired the scurrilous comment, "Amy Lowell, from left to right," the girth of the poet being a favorite subject for merriment in newspapers and elsewhere.

It was something less and more than a joke to the poet. Eventually it was her death, at the apex of her career and

powers. For nearly the whole of her life, the glandular imbalance appearing at the age of eight, it was a travesty of
her own ideals of beauty and decorum' "Lord, I'm a walking
sideshow!" she once said. And it was, most significantly,
the quietus to her hope to be loved. Suitors appeared at the
graceful portal of Sevenels, but the transactions they had
in mind were those of the marketplace. It might be said that
a prudent compromise was incumbent on the wealthy
heiress, but such language has no meaning as applied to
Amy Lowell. For her, as for her idol, Keats, love was a
sacred experience, and it was one of the signs of her greatness that she never demeaned or falsified her own nature.

As Foster Damon remarks in his biography of the poet,
the Keatsian philosophy: "the holiness of the heart's af-
fections and the truth of imagination," became virtually
her creed, but the idealism so expressed merely compounded
her loss:

> I wandered through a house of many rooms.
> It grew darker and darker,
> Until, at last, I could only find my way
> By passing my fingers along the wall.
> Suddenly my hand shot through an open window,
> And the thorn of a rose I could not see
> Pricked it so sharply
> That I cried aloud.
>
> [*CP*, 237]

III

*the most dynamic personality in modern
American poetry*

ALFRED KREYMBORG

If Amy Lowell could not demean herself to accept an un-
felt love, she could also do no less than to enact the full

drama of her spectacular nature. In considering the value of her personality, it is useful to turn to the writings of Harriet Monroe, founder of *Poetry* Magazine and close associate of Miss Lowell from the earliest days of her career.[4] Unlike certain male admirers who may have been biased, Miss Monroe saw Amy Lowell as a feminine rival and a clear threat to the prominence of the Mid-West poets which her magazine continually championed.

Accordingly, there was sporadic warfare between the two women, Amy Lowell demanding the preferential treatment of a Vachel Lindsay while Miss Monroe countered with snubs, evasions, and hostile reviews of Amy Lowell's volumes. In spite of this and much plain speech from Miss Lowell ("I am sorry to appear stiff and disagreable . . . but I admit, Harriet, that I am hurt"), the two were united by a bond of affection and mutual respect. Unfortunately, in the last months of the poet's life, Miss Monroe, unaware of her friend's state of health, administered her most serious rebuke. This took the form of a critical evaluation, the first one she ever printed on Miss Lowell, which opened in a niggling vein: "One may as well begin by granting Amy Lowell everything but genius. There is a rumor, probably too plausible to be true, that she once said, 'I made myself a poet, but the Lord made me a business man!' " Though the remainder of the essay was more genial, neither Miss Lowell nor any other reader could miss the fact that the Bostonian was being put firmly in place as a poet of minor accomplishments.

In view of these circumstances, Miss Monroe was saddened and mortified by the poet's unexpected death. There was a great deal to regret, and her first act was to put off evasion and to speak in her own voice in the reviews of the poet's three posthumous books. These are sensible reviews. Miss Monroe wishes now to see things as they are. But the surprise they contain is their insistence on the greatness of Amy Lowell; this and grief at her passing are the real themes of the essays.

It was a striking reversal. In 1928, three years after Miss

Lowell's death, the emotion is unassuaged. "One resents the power of death to snuff out so lightly the flame of an august and regnant spirit," she wrote. It was guilt which spoke, but the ring of conviction is unmistakable. Miss Monroe, who wrote astutely about her contributors, never again paid such a tribute; and her refrain "a great woman" was the view of nearly everyone who could estimate Miss Lowell fairly. These words of Henry Seidel Canby written within days of her death represent the general opinion of that time:

> But if her power over verse had been, like Dr. Johnson's, ordinary instead of extraordinary, Miss Lowell would still have been a luminous figure in this age. Her personality was in itself a *magnum opus*, and her brilliant instigations, which never deserved so gross a term as influence, have awakened the intellectual being of others as skillful as she, though never so magnificently human. She was not only poetical, but the cause of poetry in others. She, as well as her poetry, will take a place in American literature, and that is a tribute few can expect.[5]

IV

Has it not been well acted?

EMPEROR AUGUSTUS, *dying*

For accounts of Amy Lowell's preeminence we must look to her contemporaries, and their impressions are complete in regard to the outer aspects of her career. Inspired by a unique and vivid personality, a large literature of anecdote and reminiscence has accumulated around her name. This is known as the Amy Lowell "legend," but one notices that the stories usually turn out to be true. Many of the stories and most of the facts of Miss Lowell's life may be found in a biography by S. Foster Damon, a painstaking reconstruction of the events of her outer life. Unfortunately for the poet and her readers, Damon's book leaves Miss Lowell herself essentially untouched. There is a difference between the revelation of character and the recital of specific words and acts called forth by particular occasions. Of the latter, anecdotal method there is an excess in the case of Amy Lowell. It is as if one were to judge a mansion by the hangings on its walls or the pattern of its carpets. Surviving today as a miscellany of startling attributes, Amy Lowell has ceased to be the inspiriting force known to her contemporaries, while her poetry, lacking a sufficient rationale, has sunk to the status of a footnote to her career.

The mistake has been to gaze only at these outer trappings. Like "The Little Ivory Figures Pulled With a String" in one of her best poems [*CP*, 236], it was assumed that Miss Lowell had no internal organs, and a like separation was supposed to exist between her human qualities and the content of her art. In this respect, Harriet Monroe, an unmarried woman herself, was never deceived. In her review of *Ballads For Sale*, the last of the posthumous volumes, she points out the identity of poet and poetry—"always, inevitably and inescapably, she is there"—but fails to recognize the tincture of greatness this implies. Not a great poet by the standards we ordinarily apply, Miss Lowell is yet the author of some few great poems, and this as well as the radiance of the whole is the effect of a nobility of spirit.

Appearing in Philadelphia on one of her frequent lecture tours, Miss Lowell inquired about the affect of her lamp on the eyes of a lady seated in the front-row. She answered, "I see another light." So did most others who could view her without bias. If Amy Lowell was great, it was because of an imperial spirit that was as manifest as her corpulent form. She once wrote, "being a soldier, I should wish to be a general," and most observers noted her gifts for ruling others. Glenn Frank once envisioned her as president of the United States and Harriet Monroe as an eighteenth-century monarch. But this is to stress what was external in her nature and so of secondary moment in Miss Lowell's own scale of values.

Proof of her power lay rather in her inner life. It consists first in the record of her struggle against illness, a contest which began in childhood and took finally the form of the threat of imminent death from muscular strangulation. Hydra-headed in a demonic sense, one malady followed on another, the sheer number and variety of the attacks being staggering. In 1920, alone, Miss Lowell needed half of the year to recover from two unsuccessful operations.[6]. Of all this Miss Lowell took scarcely any notice. Her pace of work barely slackened and she remained undaunted in circumstances that would have ended the active lives of most persons. In 1924, having completed the exhausting labors involved in her work on Keats, she turned without pause or misgiving to other large projects, but was forestalled by death. It was a tragedy for which no one except a few intimates was prepared. At the age of fifty-one she showed few external signs of aging and her last published essay, fittingly entitled, "Open The Door," had an irresistible power and logic:

> To the Editor of the Saturday Review,
> SIR:
>   Since a flaw in a friend may not be tolerated while the same rift in an enemy is a matter of no moment whatever, I feel an irresistible need to chide you a little —yes, indeed, more than a little—for the haste or carelessness which permitted you to print the jejune and ill-digested review of Mrs. Conklin's volume of poems, *Ship's Log*, in your number of January 24th. I have no idea who wrote the review, which is unsigned, and I may be treading on the toes of some intimate friend in objecting to it, but it must be objected to in the interest of fair statement and well-con-

sidered criticism. It is quite clear that your reviewer never gained the slightest idea of the essence of the book, that she . . . brought to it a temperamental bias so inimical to the whole attitude of the poems that they remained absolutely sealed to her, and all she could think to say was that she missed a certain lyrical touch which she had found in some of Mrs. Conklin's earlier work, which touch seems inextricably bound up in her mind with the age-old patterns of rhyme and meter. And here is where I blame you, for so inelastic an individual should never have been permitted to tap with the stick of the well-intentioned blind among the flowering borders of Mrs. Conklin's verse. As an expression of opinion the review is well enough; as criticism it is an insult to the intelligence of your readers. . . .[7]

Reading Miss Lowell's words along with the tepid review which provoked them, one is struck by the disparity between the offense and its punishment. But the issue concerned was the nature and value of Imagism, whose propagation had been her life's work; and the letter reveals her as well exulting in newly gathered powers three months before her death.

V

One must aspire to be an original not a copy.
QUEEN CHRISTINA

In 1903 Amy Lowell was engaged in the first of the series of controversies which were to puctuate her career.

In a sense she had prepared herself for this by an even earlier skirmish over education in Brookline. On the latter occasion she scandalized her own family by rising at a public meeting to speak in heated tones against a school official incapacitated by age. Mistaking hisses for sounds of applause, she continued in her bare-fisted way exposing the folly of reappointing this senile man for reasons of sentiment. Stepping down from the platform, she was informed "that no woman of the Lowell family had ever spoken in public before." Nevertheless, her speech resulted in the appointment of a new official, so Miss Lowell felt herself "thoroughly justified" (Damon, 143-44). It was a hopeful start for a woman who has been described as "the most flamboyant lady in American letters."[8] As was to happen so often, she had combined the ludicrous with the high-minded, and her sense of the rightness of this was not the least of her insights.

Two years later the circumstances were nearly reversed. A majority of the directors of the Boston Athenaeum, a private library and lecture hall, had voted to demolish their aged quarters and rebuild on another site. In part the motive was to secure a large profit from the sale of the real estate on Beacon Hill. Amy Lowell, a shareholder in the institution, felt that this would be the destruction of a hallowed legacy from the past, and so would diminish the historical awareness of the Bostonians.

To plan a rescue campaign she summoned the few directors who supported her to a meeting at the home she had inherited from her father a few years before. It was a fateful moment: the first combat between Victorian correctness and a rebel who worked ceaselessly in later life to lessen its rigor. Not that the twenty-nine-year-old heiress would have viewed the meeting in any such light. At this time she was uncertain of her future, an unknown poet with no ambitions to lead others in new social or literary endeavors. As was her habit from the beginning, Amy Lowell was simply being herself.

However that may be, the experience must have been

startling for the gentlemen concerned. The hostess did not descend to her reception rooms on the ground-floor. She received her male callers from her enormous bed, clad in pajamas and with a large, black umbrella shielding her from the afternoon sun. Although it was three in the afternoon, the breakfast dishes were at her side and she was smoking a pipe. The business which had prompted the meeting was quickly dispatched. After all, Amy Lowell had called on these men only to ratify her own plan. She gave the necessary instructions, and her plan being put to the test the ancient building was saved.[9]

The same unconcern for proprieties appears in an incident involving the poet-critic Louis Untermeyer, who (at the time) had been a close friend of Miss Lowell for some years. As he tells the story in his autobiography, he and the poet were guests at a banquet honoring John Masefield at a time early in the prohibition era:

> Since, at that time, the Hotel Astor did not offer alcoholic comfort, I spent the rest of the dinner talking to Amy Lowell. At the end of it she said; "Louis, I've never heard you talk so much and so badly. I haven't the faintest idea what you've been saying—and I don't think you have either."
>
> It was not only my discomfiture she enjoyed, but her eminence. Each of the guests of honor read, spoke, or mumbled. Next to Masefield, Amy received the most applause. But she raised her hand and asked them to stop. "Just to make me feel at home," she said, "please add a few hisses. I'm not used to speaking without them." Later, when she attacked some of the enshrined poets of the past, the hissing was renewed—and this time the audience meant it.[10]

Improbable as this behavior might seem, these stories are not inventions. They are too consistent and too fully reported to allow such a suspicion.

A case in point is the account by Robert Frost of Miss Lowell's visit to Ann Arbor at the time he was serving as

poet-in-residence there. This visit coincided with the peak
of her fame, and she read her poetry to an audience of
thousands in Hill Auditorium. Though the reading was an
overwhelming success, Frost chose to emphasize certain
oddities he disliked in her behavior. His report of the encounter was contained in a letter to Untermeyer:

> May 19, 1922
> Ann Arbor
>
> Dear Louis:
>
> No, Amy didn't displace you in our affections. You
> still hold the top of both batting and fielding lists.
> Amy upset a lamp and a water pitcher and was in turn
> herself upset when I told her what you said about the
> lumber-yard on her shoulder. She called the janitor
> fool and damn fool to his face—this was out back be-
> fore she went on—and she called Conrad of the Whim-
> sies "boy" in the sense of slave. [Frost fails to mention
> that Miss Lowell apologized when Conrad was
> identified as head of the poetry club and told him "You
> may call me girl."] She and I were ten minutes before
> the whole audience disentangling the lengthener wire
> on her lamp. As a show she was more or less successful.
> After it was all over she described Straus to some ladies,
> among them Mrs. Straus, as the fussy old professor who
> stood around and didn't help. Straus says she must
> have meant me. She laid about her. And in that respect
> she disappointed nobody. She only failed to live
> up to expectations when she stole away from a house
> full of guests and came to my house to smoke her
> cigar in private. Her speaking and reading went well
> considering the uproarious start she made with the
> lamp and water. I never heard such spontaneous shouts
> of laughter. Out in front she took it all well with
> plenty of talk offhand and so passed for a first-class
> sport. . . .[11]

Unlike the crowd in the auditorium, Frost was dis-
dainful of Miss Lowell and her work. He witnessed but

did not understand her value as a liberating force: "I never heard such spontaneous shouts of laughter." But his facts were accurate and the visitor's charm could not conceal her belligerencies or the disregard for the feelings of others.

The same disregard for conventions was expressed in other activities of Miss Lowell. Having fixed upon the midnight hours to begin her working day (to protect herself from the telephone and other social importunities) she chose the hour of 2 A.M. to interrupt the sleep of friends with phone calls about literary business, doing so with seeming ease and nonchalance. Implicit in this behavior was her refusal to treat others as equals, an attitude that was also manifest in her disregard for punctuality. Amy Lowell, it seems, was never on time for anything, an interview, a small gathering, or a lecture to be given before a large audience. Guests invited to her home were required to observe a strict schedule, both in arriving and departing. But the hostess herself appeared when she chose, usually not until several courses of the dinner had been served.[12]

At the dinners part of the drama of her entrances was supplied by a herd of sheep-dogs, who stood almost in the relation of children for Miss Lowell.. The names of some of these pets were Lydia, Rosine, Mary, Columbine, Jack, John, and Tommy; and of this group Mary was the star performer and special favorite of Miss Lowell. Sometimes they would sit in dignified silence around the long, glittering table, and they always joined the guests for conversation in the library. On one such occasion, Margaret Widdemer was surprised to detect the flicker of a smile on Miss Lowell's face, as if she were amused at the circus-like gathering in front of her. Another guest felt a Circe-like atmosphere at these revels. No doubt there was a basis to these suspicions. Amy Lowell was prone to love all of her intimates and she would sit all night with a pet dog who was sick. But she did not make the mistake of overestimating either men or dogs or of failing to note resemblances. If most of her guests seemed unimpressive, this would be due first of all to their limited perceptions. The tragic fate

which had immobilized Amy Lowell in giving her a clown-
ish human form unveiled the beauty and life of things with
the same movement while setting her irrevocably beyond
their pale. The awareness she had gained in recompense
was such that most of her contemporaries did not grasp it
at all, as proved by the fact that they saw her poems mainly
as pictures of flowers.

Nor was the conjunction of man and dog altogether
misplaced. Those who smiled at her receptions turned their
backs wordlessly when the hostess died with her affairs in
serious disarray: the voluminous poetry unedited, her
place in literature challenged and undefined. Out of all
her many associates only one or two has ever defended
her value as a poet, while two biographies of a malignant
nature have never been publicly contested by her friends.
The disloyalty and shallowness which this behavior implies are weaknesses of human nature of which Miss Lowell
was keenly aware. These may well be reasons for the con-
tempt with which she often treated others. However, as
one of her friends of these years has remarked, Amy Lowell's
well known belligerence was chiefly a response to the
countless attacks which were made on her.

VI

Miscast

The gulf in habits and attitudes which separated Amy
Lowell from most other literary persons helps to explain
the lack of sympathetic attention she received after her
death when her awesome personality was removed from the
scene. But we must also explain the extraordinary fame and
influence she acquired so suddenly in the last decade of
her life. To do this we will go back again briefly to the
earlier part of her life. Although as a young woman Miss

Lowell had sometimes given signs of striking out on an
independent path, the turning point in her life did not
come until the years 1913-1914. In 1912, nearing the age
of forty, Miss Lowell published her first volume of poems.
Although this book was the product of ten years of serious
effort, it was a humiliating failure, disdainfully reviewed
by Louis Untermeyer and elsewhere virtually unsold and
unread. The same year marked the end of twenty years of
loneliness (since her appearance as a debutante whose low
point was marked by the nervous breakdown she suffered
from 1898 to 1905. Although Miss Lowell had many and
varied pastimes suited to her social position, she was a
giant fallen into chains and the inanity of polite diversions
had nothing to answer to her dreams. This is the note that
is struck in "Miscast," a poem written in 1913, antedating
her first public success but at a time when the walls around
her were visibly cracking.

I

I have whetted my brain until it is like a Damascus
    blade,
So keen that it nicks off the floating fringes of
    passers-by,
So sharp that the air would turn its edge
Were it to be twisted in flight.
Licking passions have bitten their arabesques into it,
And the mark of them lies, in and out, worm-like,
With the beauty of corroded copper patterning white
    steel.
My brain is curved like a scimitar,
And sighs at its cutting
Like a sickle mowing grass,
    But of what use is all this to me!
    I, who am set to crack stones
    In a country lane!

II.
My heart is like a cleft pomegranate
Bleeding crimson seeds
And dripping them on the ground.
My heart gapes because it is ripe and over-full,
And its seeds are bursting from it.
But how is this other than a torment to me!
I, who am shut up, with broken crockery,
In a dark closet!

[*CP*, 42]

Although "Miscast" is unappealing, it is so for a different reason than the verses collected in her unsuccessful first volume. Those poems were pallid and feeble. We have there not only the shadow of the cage but the numbness of the inmate. "Miscast," on the contrary, bristles with energy and purpose. It is an effective poem, giving a vivid account of her emotional state at this time. But what we have is Miss Lowell at her most rebellious, and for many in Boston it must have been dampening to hear the city described as "a dark closet" and its leading citizens as "broken crockery." But this is to ridicule her sentiments. The point is that the poet had advanced. She had nearly become the formidable figure known to literary annals. More precisely, she was still in process of a change that begot many novelties in the course of the two years in question.

The events of these years will be described below. Here it may suffice to say that this was the time that Miss Lowell found her own voice in poetry, creating in a short space of time a number of poems of a fresh and startling beauty. It was also the period when Miss Lowell became the leader of the Imagist group of poets, a movement which in a few years' time renewed public interest in poetry and transformed our conception of its purpose and nature (Damon, 726-27). As envisioned by Miss Lowell, the movement also carried basic social and philosophic implications of undoubted importance in the evolution of

Western life. Of all this and more Miss Lowell became the brilliant spokesman, giving a direction and meaning to the "new poetry" in America which it would have lacked without her insights and gifts of leadership (Damon, 426). In doing so, she became the foremost American poet, achieving for herself and the other new poets a fame and influence very unusual in the life of the country.

It was a commanding role, one fit to match the dreams of the giant. Sailing from England to the United States in the fall of 1913, after her first visit with the newly emerged Imagists, Miss Lowell expressed her high spirits by running things on board ship to suit herself. From this time until the moment of her death eleven years later, it was the imperial will which was to be the most conspicuous quality in Amy Lowell's life and to account for much that we find in her poetry.

VII

Metamorphosis

Once released by a sufficient challenge, this spirit swept all before it, not only in the literary world but in the inner world of Miss Lowell herself. It was the force that enabled her to dominate serious illness and, rebounding from that, to ask no less than the full realization of her selfhood. The bristling and bustling figure that comes down to us from that time was neither bizarre nor ill-assorted. It was rather that she was complex and fully exposed. The best explanation even for her truculence was that "it was there", and the "natural action" she practiced and approved implies the expression of the lower as well as the higher self. Had she been challenged it is likely she could have justified her behavior. Few literary persons whose histories are known have acted so consistently on high principles or made the sacrifices for art that she did. In this connection, it is interesting to note certain religious views which she set down in her diary at the age of fifteen. After listening to a moralistic sermon given at church, she rejected the pastor's view that one should live by a fixed code in order to insure the soul's salvation. This was only selfishness, she confided to her journal. One should do his duty and depend on the understanding of God for the rest (Damon, 93).

Although her religious ideas became more heterodox as time passed, it is not possible to account for Amy Lowell outside of a transpersonal religious framework—a set of beliefs in which she found her value and goal in labor in "the vineyards of the Lord." This is a formulation whose puritan associations she would have disapproved. But the same attitude expressed in Greek pagan terms is the theme of her poem, "Before The Altar," which she chose to open her first book of poems (*CP*, 1).

If we look at Miss Lowell in the light of these attitudes, we may see more than exhibitionism in her unflinching self-exposure, begun as a girl in her diary and completed in her poetry and life. Two poems which treat the function of the artist, her very first and one of the last, both concern the great actress, Eleonora Duse, and are suffused with a religious atmosphere of veneration and awe. What Miss Lowell saw in Duse was the quality best discribed in an essay on her by Arthur Symons: a profundity of spirit which adopts art for its own end but continually transcends it, being greater than any given artistic construct. Both Symons and Miss Lowell defined this end as the speech of the soul, that is, the delineation of personality itself, the supreme mystery of the knowable universe.[13]

It was the revelation of this possibility in art that moved Amy Lowell to become a poet. Sitting in the darkness of the Tremont Theater on the evening of October 21, 1902, she was dazzled by the power of Duse's art and was inspired to write her first poem since childhood.

"I went to see her, as I always went to see everything
that was good in the theater. The effect on me was
something tremendous. What really happened was
that it revealed me to myself, but I hardly knew that
at the time. I just knew that I had got to express the
sensations that Duse's acting gave me, somehow. I
knew nothing whatever about the technique of poetry . . . I was as ignorant as anyone could be. I sat
down, and with infinite agitation wrote this poem.
[Damon, 147-48]

In view of her handicaps and the intricacy of the subject,
the poem is surprisingly well made. What is more, it gives
a lucid account of her experience. She had discovered, with
a start, her own emotions being enacted on the stage and
had recognized the power of art to penetrate and order
the living stream of life. This was a lesson not to be learned
from the contrived and dusty emotions of the late Roman-
tics, and it was precisely what Amy Lowell needed to know.
If the imperious will demanded the full expression of the
self, a means to that end was available in art which would
render not only the appearance but the substance of life
as well:

Her voice is vibrant with a thousand things;
Is sharp with pain or choked with tears,
Or rich with love and longing.
Her little inarticulate sounds are sprung
From depths of inner meaning which embrace
A life's chaotic, vast experience . . .
And as the evening lengthens, bit by bit,
Little by little, we discern the real.
'Tis that which holds us spellbound far, far more
Than even her most consummate art can do,
Through all the passion of a simulated grief
And through the studied anquish learnt by rote
We feel the throbbing of a human soul,
A woman's heart that cries to God and fears!
[*CP*, 593]

The phrasing is trite and the emotions untidy, but this does not cancel the value of the conception. In Duse acting on a Boston stage Amy Lowell had discovered the expressionistic and revelatory powers of art.

This was the insight that galvanized Miss Lowell and gave her flagging life a purpose. What Duse had achieved on the stage she would perform in her poems and, more curiously, in her life as well. A comment of Elizabeth Sergeant, admiring friend of the poet comes to mind: "She lived dramatically, opulently, always for spectators." Miss Lowell would have been the first to admit this, having calculated her effects so carefully. And the self-offering so contrived with scant respect for convention would represent not bold self-advertisement, as some believed, but a kind of religious celebration. After all, this was what Duse herself had intended in her first triumph on the stage, when the meager and shabby adolescent had clutched a huge bouquet of flowers throughout her performance.[14]

VIII

Song for a Viola D'Amore

Writing in *Scribner's* Magazine a short time after her friend's death, Elizabeth Perkins has given us an invaluable glimpse of the mystical tendency of Amy Lowell's thought.[15] This was not an attitude she adopted as an ornamental dress becoming to the role of poet nor was it anything that Miss Lowell ever cultivated (unlike Yeats) or publicly professed. It was rather the shape of her mind that could not content itself in any of the ready-made categories of thought offered by religion and philosophy. If the poet was exceptional in her personal habits, she was even more extended in her mental life which flowed, through hidden channels, into nearly every mode of existence. This is the meaning of an observation by John Lowes concerning her treatment of external nature:

> Precisely what is Amy Lowell or Li T'ai Po, I neither know nor greatly care. But I do know that she has taken things of beauty which to their readers for centuries were (as they felt them) 'like Spring flowers', 'like the branches of trees reflected in water—the branches of still trees', and through her unison with their spirit has recreated their delicate, lingering charm.[16]

The words one should note are "through her unison with their spirit." Though still trees and spring flowers may seem unimpressive to some, it is the possibility of the transfer of consciousness and not its objects which interests us. So we have Debussy's recreation of the ocean in *La Mer* and Miss Lowell gives us her striking evocations of the earth and sky.

It is only in terms of these largest motions of the mind that the reader can approach the inner fastness of Miss Lowell's emotional life. However, the question remains whether this should be done at all since it involves feelings of the most private kind. Here, the choice has been taken from the hands of the scholar. Amy Lowell was not content with anything less than a full record of her inner life, and, being passionate, the poetry of love and desire occupy a large place in her writings. To overlook or minimize this would be to falsify her work and to strike at one of its principal values, its sturdy self-revelation.

We have noted the part played in this by the will to self-completion. It may be added here that so much was projected because other possibilities were so few. For Amy nearly the whole vital center of life could be realized only through the imaginative processes of art, so that a large part of her work must be interpreted in this light. This is especially true of the poems expressing erotic interest in women. It is a conspicuous theme and there is no reason to see in it the operation of a poetic mask or persona. In any event, this type of emotional fabrication would be contrary to the confessional spirit of her work, whose subject matter, she insisted once, always originated in unconscious impulses (Damon, 630).

The explanation would seem to be more obvious and also more complex. It *was* an area of genuine sensibility in Miss Lowell, and one that was inseparable from the power of apprehension by which the artist can order and possess the external world. If the artist is an eye, it is an eye that must see whole; if a spirit, not the half but the two halves of the divided being always seeking reunion and completion in the ancient Greek myth. It is not more than is implied in the dramas of Shakespeare, who lived equally in Duke Orsino and the fluttering Viola, in Romeo and the loving Juliet.[17] If objection is made to the predominance of the male impulse in the work of Miss Lowell, then the same stricture would apply in reverse to Henry James, who was never fully himself except in inhabiting and expressing the female sensibility. The subject could be expanded indefinitely, including the preference of many male artists for fierce, Amazonian consorts.[18] The point is that the artist is a world, and a world is populated by many shapes of thought and desire.

In the early youth of Amy Lowell a soreness of feeling on this account is evident in the diary which she wrote in her sixteenth and seventeenth years, and it is, without doubt, the subject of the agonized late poem, "The Green Parakeet," whose theme is sexual guilt. However, the early girlhood diary reveals that Miss Lowell, like most other persons, expected and sought her happiness in marriage. The evidence of her life is still more illuminating. Miss Lowell had powerful attachments to two women, Eleonora Duse and Ada Russell, and in her poems she has described them in terms of the most exceptional beauty. Yet both of these women were past middle age when Amy met them and neither was graced with comeliness of face or form. Remarkable as this may seem, the poet never noticed the fact. What she saw and loved in these women was a spiritual beauty—which, of course, removed the relationships to a rare and platonic plane.

However one may view the emotions of the poet, what counts for us is their contribution to her art. Like her contemporary, the American painter Mary Cassatt, Miss Lowell was sensitive to a thousand tones, gestures, and nuances in the female, and we must be grateful that she was able to articulate these in subtle images of femininity. One of the best is the late poem, "Song For A Viola D'Amore," an impression of Mrs. Russell in which bodily form is all but dissolved in a symbolism of ineffable beauty:

> The lady of my choice is bright
> As a clematis at the touch of night,
> As a white clematis with a purple heart
> When twilight cuts earth and sun apart.
> Through the dusking garden I hear her voice
> As a smooth, sweet, wandering, windy noise,
> And I see her stand as a ghost may do
> In answer to a rendezvous
> Long sought with agony and prayer.
> So watching her, I see her there.
>
> I sit beneath a quiet tree
> And watch her everlastingly.
> The garden may or may not be
> Before my eyes, I cannot see.
> But darkness drifting up and down
> Divides to let her silken gown
> Gleam there beside the clematis.
> How marvelously white it is!
> Five white blossoms and she are there
> Like candles in a fluttering air
> Escaping from a tower starr.
>
> *Be still you cursed, rattling leaf,*
> *This is no time to think of grief. . . .*

[*CP*, 443-44]

IX

Patterns

When Amy Lowell died suddenly on a May afternoon while great shocks of lilac bloom punctuated the contours of her estate, her niece, hastily summoned, bared the mystery of the vault in Miss Lowell's great, high-ceilinged library. The instructions she found were for an austere and decorous final arrangement of things. All that was unformed, personal, of the moment only or only of the flesh was disowned. The body of the poet was to be cremated, there was to be no religious service, and only the immediate family would be present for the private burial at Mount Auburn. The poet who had scrupulously burned all preliminary drafts of her poems now asked that all unfinished work be consigned to the flames. It was the last assertion of the imperial will, a set of proceedings drastically at variance with the customs of her family, and the expression above all of her aristocratic spirit.

While the revelatory nature of Duse's art led Amy Lowell in the opposite direction, that is, toward expansion and personal expression, it was the force of the aristocratic ideal which gave such "clean and polished" shape to nearly every act of her outer life. It was again that central tension in her life, expressed in many different forms, but most often as the rebellion of the heart against external constraints. This attitude was given its classic expression in "Patterns," one of the best known recent American poems. However, what is usually overlooked in this poem is the fact that its appeal is derived not from an opposition of black and white but a conflict of rival values of almost equal appeal and validity. It is not only the garden that is beautiful, because of its strictness of design, but the heroine herself has been translated into a "rare pattern" of jewels and brocade as she sweeps proudly along the garden-paths.

It is this image that holds the reader more than the nude-bathing introduced later, essential as that is to the design of the poem. By a marvelous economy, Miss Lowell's sharp cry of pain is also the best possible case that can be made for those restrictive eighteenth-century graces. Bathing in public without clothes one asserts the rightful claims of the body. Miss Lowell might do this in her poems but she understood very well that in her own life, with its tragic limitations, salvation and personal distinction could come only through attachment to great universals, and what better avenue to this than the aristocratic code, seized at its heroic, self-denying end! Born a noble by inner character, these qualities were fostered in her by the standards and frame of life offered by an American "ruling family."[19]

X

The Castle: 1874-1912

Amy Lowell was born on February 9, 1874, in Brookline, Massachusetts, a suburb of Boston. The family into which she was born had settled in New England in 1639 and had been prominent in its affairs for nearly five generations. At the time of the American Revolution there had been a sharp accession in the influence and fortunes of the Lowells and this was balanced in the nineteenth century by the rise to industrial over-lordship of the great grand-uncle, grandfather, and the father of Miss Lowell. Not long after Amy's birth in the forty-fifth year of her father's life, Augustus had become the president or other chief officer of twenty cotton mills and banks. But the wealth this activity created was never destined to remain long in business hands. Though they had proved themselves exceedingly astute in the management of worldly affairs, the predilection of the Lowells was for the life of the mind and the cultivation of humane values. John Lowell II, great great grandfather of the poet, had been among the first in America to give serious attention to scientific farming and horticulture, and it was this gentleman who first laid out the gardens of Bromley Vale, an estate in Roxbury which served as "county seat" for the Lowells until late in the nineteenth century. The fortune of his son, the industrial pioneer, Francis Cabot, was devoted to the purpose of adult education, the lecture courses of the Lowell Institute becoming an immediate success upon their inauguration in 1840 by Amy's grandfather.

However great this man's liberality of mind (he was the founder of a "utopian" workers' community at Lowell, Massachusetts), he would never have recognized the most brilliant of the Lowells in the flaxen-haired daughter of Augustus, eight years old at the time of the patriarch's death. In fact, the idea would have astonished the child herself. Entrusted to the care of an older sister, because of the invalid state of Mrs. Lowell, there was little to distinguish the childhood of the poet except an uncommon quickness of mind and a self-assertion partly choked by the stiff proprieties of a Victorian household. The blighting effect of this atmosphere created by the personality of Augustus has been well described by Elizabeth Perkins, a girlhood friend, who speaks of the "Unaccustomed terror" that fell upon her "when a portfolio left on a forbidden table or arrival . . . five minutes late for breakfast shadowed the hospitable spirit of the house and lowered the temperature."[20]

This coldness and rigor of spirit of Augustus may well be connected with the serious nervous illnesses suffered by his wife, the delicate Katherine Lawrence, and three of his five children, Percival, Katherine, and Amy. However that may be, it is a fact that the first noteworthy event in Amy Lowell's life showed an unusual proneness to nervous disturbances. Taken on a summer's visit to Europe, the family galloped through Scotland, England, France,

Belgium, Holland, Italy, Germany, Norway, Denmark, and Sweden "at a fearful rate of speed." The effect of this pace was totally unexpected. Overstimulated by the sights and the rapid change of scene, the eight-year-old child became "fearfully ill." Taken to see torture devices at Nuremburg, "for months afterwards," she wrote, "my nights were made horrible by visions of the Iron Virgin. The return home, however, and the tranquil life which ensued, averted what I think might easily have been a serious nervous breakdown. . . although it was many years before I recovered my nerve and ceased to be afraid of the dark" (Damon, 49-51).

Taken at its face value, the account suggests special sensitivities that would be of value to a poet. On the other hand, it may be possible to connect this nervous derangement with the physical disorder that appeared a short time later: that is, to posit an emotional causation for her lifelong glandular imbalance. Attending a party not long after her return from Europe, Amy was challenged by a brother to eat an extra plate of rice—"she did, but when they prepared to go home, her coat would not button across her stomach, 'And it never buttoned again,' Miss Lowell said, describing the episode" (Damon, 51). The stoutness thus described became more pronounced with the passage into youth and adulthood, the young lady of thirty-four weighing two hundred and forty-eight pounds at the time of her Middle Eastern travels with her beautiful friend, Barbara Higginson.

These were real calamities, but one must not suppose that this is the whole story of Amy Lowell's childhood. Sevenels, with its woodland, meadow, stables, and gardens, was a muchly loved playground; and as the pampered darling of aging parents she had many pleasures and privileges to enjoy. Among the first of these was the authority conferred on her by being born a Lowell, a fact of which the poet was always keenly aware. In the same year that the child traveled in Europe, this prestige was enhanced by the marriage of Amy's sister, Katherine, to Alfred Roosevelt, the first cousin of the future president. In later years, this alliance seemed to please Miss Lowell, much more so than the marriage of her cousin, Mary, to the English Earl of Berkeley.

As for education this was the lightest of burdens and there were many serious deficiencies since Augustus believed that advanced education should be reserved for males. When Amy was nine years old, her English governess, who left her with a life-long inability to spell, was replaced by classes in private schools. However, being quicker and bolder than her teachers, she was a terror to them: "a child precocious, well informed, a tom-boy, quick at retort, spoiled, and impatient at drudgery." The "ringleader in fun and mischief," she was regularly passed from one school to another. A fitting epitaph for the period was the despairing comment of a French teacher: "Ne riez pas des betises d'Aimee" (Damon, 56).

But this phase of her life was essentially negative, the failure to find the discipline and intellectual sustenance she required. Because Amy was between generations, it was her older sister, Elizabeth, who took responsibility for the child, and Bessie was a less forceful personality than her charge. On the other hand, there was much to be gained from the examples set by her brothers, Percival and Lawrence, nineteen and eighteen years old, respectively, at the time of her birth. In the case of Percival, the contribution was decisive. When this gifted adventurer took up residence in Japan, 1883-1893, the stream of "pictures, prints, and kakemonos" which flowed in on the child at home became a dominant influence in her esthetic development and was partly responsible for molding her own verse in later years. Percival contributed in other ways as well. The mental horizon which she expanded in Europe in 1882, and on the trip she took across the continent to California the following year was completed for Amy in the outpost which Percy established in Japan, the four books which he wrote at this time being a searching investigation of Oriental life. By the standards of bourgeois Boston, or nearly any others of that time, hers was a royal view, and it was amplified by the many studies and travels she undertook later.

In the decade that followed this travel and in the years of her early youth, what was most decisive for Amy was what did not happen. The pert and authoritarian child grew into a disadvantaged adolescent and young woman. On the spring-board floor of Papanti's, the dancing school for the fashionable, she was a zestful dancer, but the square-faced and overweight girl did not attract partners. Her sense of loss and humiliation is expressed in her diary entries at this time: "I would enjoy parties very well if I didn't have to air my sweetness in the vicinity of the wall," and the real purpose of the journal is to give vent to her forebodings of life-long loneliness, on the one hand, and on the other, to her overmastering need for love: "I think that to be married to a sweet, tender, strong and good man would be the nearest approach to perfect happiness. . . . To be his sole and whole confidante—in short my ideas of what a husband should be are very exalted. No, I shall be an old maid, nobody could love me I know. Why, if I were somebody else, I should hate myself."[21]

The tone of this is airy but the sixteen-year old girl was not always capable of such control. As time passed her entries became more and more agitated and they broke off completely at a moment of crisis produced by an un-requited love. One year later her formal education ceased and Miss Lowell came out into Boston society. But this elaborate ritual—sixty dinners were given in her honor that same season—only emphasized her anomalous posi-tion. The same was true in her other life, the life of the mind. Until well past the turn of the century when she reached the age of twenty-six, the intellectual activities of Miss Lowell were unimpressive and undefined. They were simply the attention to polite letters that might be expected of any intelligent New Englander, and the stories and verses she produced, beginning as a small child, were sporadic creations that ceased entirely at the age of nine-teen.

During these same years Miss Lowell was also overtaken

by serious personal trials. After a long illness that shadowed her daughter's life, Katherine Lowell died in 1895,
leaving Amy as hostess of Sevenels. Before taking up these
duties Miss Lowell traveled extensively in Europe, discovering a special affinity for Naples and Venice at this
time. One year later with a party of five, she commanded
a seventy-five foot yacht on a three-month cruise to the
temples of the Nile, ending with a week at the site of Abu
Simbel (Damon, 121-37). Returning to Boston in the
spring of 1898, she was stricken once more with a nervous
illness—"the real thing," she wrote later, "the kind where
you live with a perpetual headache and the slightest
sound jars you all over" (Damon, 138).

Her attack of neurasthenia was to last more than seven
years, and in this reduced state Miss Lowell retired first
to a fruit ranch in California and then to the moderate
climate of the southwest coast of England. This was the
summer of 1899 and her father died in June of the following
year. Though Miss Lowell was now independent, the
moment was not propitious for change. She was too
feeble in nerves and body to avail herself of her new oppor-
tunities. This fact is evident in her stewardship of Sevenels.
Though the young woman was now mistress of $80,000
a year (the equivalent of $300,000 or more in present-day
values), she did nothing to alter its rustic and Victorian
character. It was not until 1906 when her health had
improved that she remodeled the reception rooms of her
mansion to reflect her own taste and to harmonize with
the splendid park and gardens.

But this beauty and splendor seemed only to mock her.
In one of the many slurs he includes in his biography of the
poet, Horace Gregory remarks that the fame of Miss Lowell
will rest on the graceful letters *which were written to her*
by the novelist D. H. Lawrence. Yet there is little in these
letters to compare with the literary qualities of the travel
notes which Amy herself wrote from Egypt to her father
shortly before he died. She was concerned to please him
on an excursion he did not approve—and little could sur-

pass the clarity and justness of her descriptions of the desert country. If these years of early maturity, 1900 to 1912, are bare of notable accomplishment, it was not from a lack of gifts but from a fundamental disorientation of her nature. To what extent her condition was due to the "unconscious oppression" of her father, the puritan "doubly distilled," cannot be known, but it is significant that Miss Lowell felt very strongly that Augustus "haunted" her library because his funeral was held there.

Recovery from the nervous collapse of 1898 was long delayed and traces of the weakness remained with her the rest of her life. The most important single advance was the experience of 1902 when Miss Lowell discovered her role as poet in watching a stage performance by Duse. But this self-discovery did not eventuate immediately in a literary career. Instead, it was followed by a long period of study and apprenticeship which ended only in 1912. While this effort was going forward, at home and among the dusty books of the Athenaeum, Miss Lowell gradually expanded her life to reflect her own unpuritan tastes and interests.

One of her first successes was the remodeling of Sevenels, the dour, Victorian décor giving way to airy, eighteenth century rooms, well suited for dancing, private concerts, and theatricals. In 1907, she began to entertain frequently and this led to the staging of plays at Sevenels. Miss Lowell herself appeared in the leading role of a play by Oscar Wilde, after which there was dancing in the hall and music room. Somewhat later, in 1910-1911, Miss Lowell joined a little theater group in Boston as actress, director, and translator of French plays (Damon, 159). But she was already in her late thirties at this time, and it was playing at "what might have been" for one of her tastes and vitality.

The same remark applies to her infatuation with the high spirited and risqué *Merry Widow* operetta which she saw seventeen times in 1908 in the company of Barbara Higginson. Like the trip these two friends took to the Mediterranean that same year, it was a farewell to a golden youth Miss Lowell had never known. By 1912, when she was preparing her first book for publication, Miss Lowell's life had moved into deeper channels and soon there would be no time for worldly diversions. Not that Miss Lowell would ever be staid or lacking in humor. Disembarking at Constantinople in 1908, she saw a trunk of her under-drawers drop into the Bosporus, the rope being snapped by the weight of these dense, canvas-like garments. Seizing the dramatic moment, she trumpeted to the throng; "My drawers, what am I going to do without my drawers!"

Chapter Two

Transcendentalism Again

Early Poems: 1902-1912

I

Four lines from a poem by Amy Lowell have been carved in stone on the face of an imposing public library.[1] This would not have surprised the poet. Miss Lowell believed firmly in the value of her work, but she would have smiled at the fact that the lines were taken from "The Boston Athenaeum," one of the first poems she wrote, a good panegyric but written in a conventional style that gives no hint of the character of her mature work. The passage concerned, which is italicized below, is interesting as an expression of Miss Lowell's elevated view of literature and for the issue it raises of the double nature of the artist: the outer man known to his contemporaries and the more valuable inner self found mainly in his work. Of equal interest for those who would judge Miss Lowell fairly is her conviction expressed in the opening lines below concerning the necessity for a sympathetic audience without which the poet's message cannot be absorbed.

. . . And as in some gay garden stretched upon
A genial southern slope, warmed by the sun
The flowers give their fragrance joyously
To the caressing touch of the hot noon;
So books give up the all of what they mean
Only in a congenial atmosphere,
Only when touched by reverent hands, and read
By those who love and feel as well as think.
For books are more than books, they are the life,
The very heart and core of ages past,
The reason why men lived, and worked, and died,
The essence and quintessence of their lives.

And we may know them better, and divine
The inner motives whence their actions sprang,
Far better than the men who only knew
Their bodily presence, the soul forever hid
From those with no ability to see.
They wait here quietly for us to come
And find them out and know them for our friends;
These men who toiled and wrote only for this,
To leave behind such modicum of truth
As each perceived and each alone could tell . . . .

[CP, 22]

The verse is effective in its very modesty and bareness of
statement, the fluid pentameter lines taking the character
of a transparent medium for the unrehearsed thought of
the author. Her thought as expressed in the poem as a
whole is a mystical identification with the history and
progress of her Anglo-American race and is best described
in the italicized line below from the conclusion of the
poem. What is at stake in the preservation of the ancient
quarters of the Athenaeum is, she says;

A sentiment profound, unsoundable,
Which Time's slow ripening alone can make
And man's blind foolishness so quickly mar.

Emotions such as these are unfathomable, but it is the
virtue of this poem that it gives concrete form to states
of mind that are otherwise nebulous and elusive.

The Athenaeum controversy and Miss Lowell's success in saving the building have been described in chapter
one. The words written to save an old library in Boston
have been engraved on the facade of a modern one in Toledo. The story illustrates the public aspect of Miss
Lowell's life, as arbiter and protector of humane values. It
was a hereditary, family role she was happy to fulfill but
which, as she reminds us in the passage quoted above,
should not be confused with the inner or essential self.

For most persons there was a special difficulty in attending to the inner side of Miss Lowell's nature. The obstacle consisted in the extraordinary amount of "surface" in her life, surface of a kind that is widely coveted and seemed to dazzle almost everyone who came in sight of the towering mansard roofs and colonnaded portal of Sevenels. Contrary to her own disclaimers,[2] this brick and stone mansion was a handsome structure whose tranquil classic grace lent itself easily to the profusion of plant forms about it and gave order and dignity to some thirty rooms, the larger of which were "state" apartments. Beginning with the reception room with its vaulted ceiling and parian marble fireplace, where one might see Miss Lowell's blue Monet, these rooms stretched in lustrous splendor ending in the vast space of a library where crystal chandeliers, hand-carved paneling, paintings, and white flowers "bloomed in a soft light."[3] This library-drawing room with its fireplaces and opulent cushioned ease was the setting of Miss Lowell's soirées and her office as well, since she wrote her poems seated at a desk near an entrance to the room. In the outer wall not far from this were French doors opening on a stone terrace, a half-way point, like the solarium on the opposite side of the house to the extensive gardens.

In this case the surface involved was nearly ten acres, so well planned, according to Miss Lowell, that "Few people, wandering round the meandering paths, under the great trees" could guess the modest proportions of the grounds. In the latter part of her life, Miss Lowell was generally confined indoors because of ill-health, but in childhood she was robust and active, and this expanse of lawn, flower beds and woodland paths was the true setting of her life, an influence as vivid and formative as any human bond, and opening another path to the hidden nature of things.

However, those who called at Sevenels were not inclined to look below surfaces or to engage in any sort of study of the poet's circumstances. Arriving on foot or in Miss Lowell's long limousine, the visitor's first impression would have been the semi-official character of her domain, an impression re-inforced by the elaborate ritual Amy Lowell imposed on her household. Foster Damon, a frequent guest at Sevenels, has described her "literary evenings" in a way that allows one to separate the shell of institutionalism from the inner core of meanings:

> While rumors about her strange life were being relayed outward through the city, from the confidences of a few old friends . . . Miss Lowell was quietly cultivating the acquaintance of most of the intelligence of America . . . . Her guests, if they did not command an automobile, took the blue Chestnut Hill car, and got off at the reservoir stop at Heath Street . . . . There they found a man waiting, who walked behind them and spoke to the sheepdogs, who came bounding ferociously through the trees of the park. Presently they saw the house with the Genoese statue of Flora above the doorway. When they were admitted, they were shown into the stiff, yellow reception-room on the right . . . . They were invited for seven . . . but not until eight o'clock did Mrs. Russell enter and lead the guests into the dining-room . . . .
>
> The dinner was an old-fashioned one, with oysters, soup, fish, meat, salad, dessert, and fruit. . . . At some point in the meal (usually after the roast had been removed) footsteps and a voice were heard; the seven sheep-dogs began barking; and while all the men rose, Miss Lowell made her hearty entrance. . . . The dogs obediently charged in the doorway, never venturing beyond the sill; hands were shaken; then the meal continued, while the vanished courses reappeared, miraculously fresh, for Miss Lowell's consumption. Although she usually had two plates of soup and was always the center of conversation, the dessert was served to all simultaneously. Then, after peppermints and ginger were passed, the party proceeded into the geniality of the library.

Before all were settled, a certain ritual was gone through. On the lamp shades Miss Lowell hung, in a certain order, the light-shields (silhouettes of children playing in enormous flowers and twigs by Lucy Morse). Then with pitch-pine splinters, Miss Lowell lighted the fire of four-foot logs, split to four-inch diameter. . . . Cigars and cigarettes were produced; coffee and liqueurs were passed. Presently she was settled with her cigar in the corner of the sofa to the right of the fireplace. . . . Glasses of water were set round. And the conversation resumed.

The flavor of those conversations can never be communicated. . . . She could talk brilliantly on any subject. Her tale might be nothing at all—how a bird was building a nest in her portico; or how she would direct traffic if she were a traffic cop. . . . But whatever it was, the company was kept in gales of helpless laughter. Yet nobody ever felt that she monopolized the conversation, for she made an excellent listener. Whatever a person's chief interest, she was eager to learn all about it; whether bayonet-drill, or the construction of lighthouses, or aviation, she asked questions and ventured opinions until she was satisfied she had mastered the essentials for herself. Meanwhile her informant heard himself talking more brilliantly than he had ever talked before. . . . If her opinions were on matters within her own ken, she retained them stubbornly at times, and enjoyed a hot skirmish. But the heat always vanished immediately when the subject was changed; she could not possibly resent honest difference of opinion . . . .

Extremely kind-hearted though she was, there was one thing she really disliked: insincerity or affectation of any sort. Poets often acquire poses in self-defense; and it was miraculous how she could pierce through those falsities to whatever was genuine underneath. She talked with such sympathy and intelligence about their work, or about poetry in general, that they forgot their attitudinizing completely. They read their poems to her, quarreled maybe with her criticisms (she felt her efforts were wasted if they acquiesced politely), and went away with a strange feeling of exhilaration. . . .

[Damon, 264-67]

The last streetcar for Boston left at 12:15 A.M. Mrs. Russell, having retired earlier in the evening, Miss Lowell saw her guests to the door at midnight and returned to the library and her own train of thought. In the meantime, what had transpired in the four-hour interval had to do only incidentally with the formality and luxury of the setting. The oracle had descended, in appropriate surroundings, and fueling her guests had herself been fueled by the interchange. In the account that Damon gives, Miss Lowell is not only one who inspires, she is also one who is able to penetrate surfaces—so that the fuller meaning of these occasions at Sevenels may be described as search parties conducted by Miss Lowell, one of the means by which she overcame the narrow limits of her highly disciplined life.

This same duality—appearance versus spirit—exists in the poet's relation to nature, known to her chiefly in the grounds of her estate. What might appear to the unwary as mere display was in fact a way station to an enlarged awareness. Whatever formal qualities Sevenels possessed by virtue of the "smooth lawns and patterned gardens" set out in 1800, these were simply the extension or reordering of the varied life of the wilderness that existed before civilization and released now in wide spaces open to the light filled these with the incessant movement of wings and the sharp, penetrant sounds of bird-song.

This aspect of Sevenels as summary of nature underlies Miss Lowell's description of it written for *Touchstone* in 1920. Filling a corner formed by two roads, she wrote, the land rose through woodland and meadow to a broad terrace skirting the house, the grass margins of which opened to the south to form a sunken garden and to the north, a small basin of water. Extending outward from this in two arms were the principal gardens and plantations of the estate, the flowering trees and shrubs, the pines, the fruit orchard and hot beds, the "old-fashioned arbour covered with wistaria and trumpet-vine."

Not so stately as a palace ground, Sevenels was more condensed and, above all, more natural. For one who could grasp its meanings, it was a mentor that whispered the insight which is always at the center of her poetry: Why this extravagant tissue of beauties to fulfill the cycles of nature unless the beauty itself defines our being and not the apparent transiency? The transcendental viewpoint implied here was the underlying motif of the poet's Imagistic work, just as it forms the explicit subjectmatter of her first collection of poems, *A Dome of Many Coloured Glass*, a title she took from Shelley's poem, "Adonais."

> Life, like a dome of many-coloured glass,
> Stains the white radiance of Eternity.

Although it is the practice to dismiss this first book as derivative and feeble, a more considered view would fix on its value as a direct statement of attitudes which inspired the content of nearly the whole of her mature work. The outer forms and modes of expression she used here were borrowed from Romantic poets such as Coleridge and Keats, but it is Amy Lowell, apprentice poet, who speaks through them. As deeply original as she was unsystematic in thought, Miss Lowell was incapable of the passive acceptance of the beliefs or philosophy of others. For this reason the propositions that she makes in *A Dome* should be viewed as independent perceptions, the result of two decades of mature reflection. The ideas that she expresses here are important as her articles of faith, as well as being the soil and nourishment of her verse. According to Foster Damon there is no record of the date Miss Lowell left the Anglican Church, but this was early in her life, well before the writing of the poems in *A Dome*. In leaving her church she was following the example of her brother, Percival, who had become a noted astronomer and free-thinker after returning from his studies in Japan. However, Amy never followed Percival in adopting the straitjacket of scientific determinism, which appears so oddly in the writings of this perceptive man. In turning from conventional Christianity and the two thousand year accumulation of churchly dogma, she was opening the door to a personal religious awareness. Though never a finished philosophy, the perceptions she made sustained her all of her life and gained greater authority as her experience deepened. This may be seen in the poem, "The Slippers of the Goddess of Beauty," an addition at the end of her life to the directly stated religious poems of 1912. It is the last treatment of her favored theme of the divinity of beauty, and here so the reader cannot mistake her meaning, the two fictional characters speak directly of an experience of the Divine so overpowering that it all but deranges their senses. The humorous framework in which the poem is set and the vividness of the sensations described—"bright pain stabbing my head"—add poignancy to this statement. However much, she says, the tone of our lives is set by ordinary concerns, represented in the poem by the colloquial banter, man's allegiance is, first of all, to the Divine and to the effort to see it "a little more, and bear to see." One should not of course be surprised in a poet of Miss Lowell's character that she has envisaged her Divinity in the form of a pagan goddess whose sandals have the distracting effect of clattering as she walks:

> *"It is easy, like Momus, to find fault*
> *with the clattering of the slipper worn*
> *by the Goddess of beauty; but 'the serious*
> *Gods' found better employment in admiration*
> *of her unapproachable loveliness."*

They clatter, clatter, clatter on the floor
Her slippers clack upon the marble slabs,

And every time her heels clap, I count one,
And go on counting till my nerves are sick
With one and one and one told out in claps.
He shot a hand out, clutching at my arm
With bony fingers. "Young man", said he, "look up.
Is that a starry face, or am I blind?
Do stars beset her like a crown of pearls?
Does sunset tinge and tangle in her hair,
And moonlight rush in silver from her breasts?
Look well, young man, for maybe I am blind."

I looked and agony assailed my brain.
He chirruped at me. "So—so! Ancient eyes
Know better than to keep upon the floor.
What dazzles you is kindly sight to me.
One gets accustomed. But I interrupt
Your count. What figure had you reached?" I shook
Him off and staggered to my room, bright pain
Stabbing my head.
            I've never found that count,
Nor started on another. Every day
I look a little longer when she comes,
And see a little more, and bear to see.
But that queer man I've never met again,
Nor very much desired to, perhaps.
Gratitude is an irksome thing to youth.
And I, thank Hermes, am still reckoned young,
Though old enough to look above the floor,
Which is a certain age, I must admit,
But I'll endure that, seeing what it brings.

                                                [*CP*, 471]

II

Before the Altar

Looking "above the floor," or transcendence of mundane concerns, was the dominant element in Amy Lowell's life. We have already seen its effects in the quality of her life at Sevenels, once described by a friend as essentially "the abode of an artist." Working its way through the worldly and materialist values of her social class and time, this urge took form in an outlook and a style of life sharply at variance with the antique Victorianism of her Boston neighbors. Not the least of her eccentricities was her decision to defy nature by working through the night and retiring at dawn, a proceeding which imposed virtual silence and restricted movement on a household of some fourteen retainers—until the princess awoke in her aeirial and sunfilled chamber at 2 P.M. This large, square room with its long dormer windows was set at the top of the house which in turn was built on a rise of ground overlooking the southerly slope of Miss Lowell's park and gardens. Because of this feature of the room, its location above the trees and access to aerial vistas, she called it Sky Parlour as a child and so anticipated the future direction of her thought.

It was a view into nature and beyond. Painstaking though they might be, the gardeners who worked in the sunken garden below could only enhance the bounty of nature and the impression for the poet was of a supernal artistry and splendor. From Sky Parlour she entered this world as through a gate, and she could, while still living in urban and industrial America, make it her occasional refuge. This is the sense of the poem, "The Matrix," which images both the values of America which she rejects as well as the inner life she affirms.

Goaded and harassed in the factory
That tears our life up into bits of days
Ticked off upon a clock which never stays,
Shredding our portion of Eternity,
We break away at last, and steal the key
Which hides a world empty of hours; ways
Of space unroll; and Heaven overlays
The leafy, sun-lit earth of Fantasy.
Beyond the ilex shadow glares the sun,
Scorching against the blue flame of the sky.
Brown lily-pads lie heavy and supine
Within a granite basin, under one
The bronze-gold glimmer of a carp; and I
Reach out my hand and pluck a nectarine.

[*CP*, 15]

Though it wobbles for a moment in lines six and seven,
the sonnet is a vigorous statement of its theme, giving first
a sharp sense of violation—"Goaded and harassed in the
factory/That tears our life up into bits of days"—and
then emotional release in a paradisal garden. The latter
is boldly visualized in a passage similar to later Imagist
writings which utilize well chosen detail to evoke the
essential quality of a scene. This poem, along with "The
Fruit-Garden Path" and other such verses from *A Dome*,
shows that the Imagist mode which Miss Lowell adopted
later was a development of qualities already present in her
poetry rather than something imposed on her work from
the outside as some critics have maintained.

Through the technique of "The Matrix" is consistent
with her best work, the same cannot be said for the ideal of
life she expresses here. There is clearly an increase of
awareness; the battered self is put in touch with a paradisal
order, but the furthest reach of her thought, in plucking
the nectarine, seems to be a simple grasping at the joys of
the senses. But this was only a momentary lapse—belied
even here by the cosmic perspective of the poem, and it is
clearly opposed to the mainstream of her life and thought.

As she tells us in one or two poems, Miss Lowell worked at night not to indulge in sensuous fantasies but to commune with a spirit she sensed in the life below her windows and even more so—in the early poems—in the appearance and movements of heavenly objects.[4] Her need for communion and worship is a theme of many poems in *A Dome,* but it is expressed most fully in the poem that opens the volume and serves as motto for the whole. In this connection one should also note that her title epitomizes the attitude she elaborates in her earliest work.

Before the Altar

Before the Altar, bowed, he stands
With empty hands;
Upon it perfumed offerings burn
Wreathing with smoke the sacrificial urn.
Not one of all these has he given,
No flame of his has leapt to Heaven
Fire-souled, vermilion-hearted,
Forked, and darted,
Consuming what a few spare pence
Have cheaply bought, to fling from hence
In idly-asked petition.

The lines are dry and stiffly written. This was Miss Lowell's first venture into free verse, and what she has done is merely to break down a metrical pattern instead of creating a new rhythm. In one sense, however, the angularity and inertness of form serve to heighten the sense of deprivation which she is expressing. After she has set her scene in this opening passage, stanza two describes the poverty of the worshipper and introduces the image of the moon which she procedes to address in the following verses of the poem:

Shining and distant Goddess, hear my prayer
Where you swim in the high air!
With charity look down on me,
Under this tree,
Tending the gifts I have not brought,
The rare and goodly things
I have not sought.
Instead, take from me all my life!
Upon the wings
Of shimmering moonbeams
I pack my poet's dreams
For you.
My wearying strife,
My courage, my loss,
Into the night I toss
For you.
Golden Divinity,
Deign to look down on me
Who so unworthily
Offers to you:
All life has known,
Seeds withered unsown,
Hopes turning quick to fears,
Laughter which dies in tears.
The shredded remnant of a man
Is all the span
And compass of my offering to you.

Empty and silent, I
Kneel before your pure, calm majesty.
On this stone, in this urn
I pour my heart and watch it burn,
Myself the sacrifice; but be
Still unmoved: Divinity.

From the altar, bathed in moonlight,
The smoke rose straight in the quiet night.

[*CP*, 1]

The poem lacks the compression and quality of image found in "The Matrix" but its thought is lucid and fully developed. Attending closely to the sense of the words, we may overlook the poem's clumsiness in favor of its revelation of Miss Lowell's nature. The subject that is treated is experience of the Divine, and this is conceived not as the mindless force of science but as a Sacred Presence. It is also clear that the experience described is real for the speaker; it is not simply the poetization of vague sentiments. Her objects of contemplation are intangible essences, not accessible to the senses, and perhaps not available to many persons at all. "For none can go beyond what he has known/And none can feel what was not felt before" is a major theme in the early poems,[5] and signifies Miss Lowell's awareness that knowing is resembling. What is *outside* can only be grasped if it is potentially existent in the mind. In these verses the poet-worshipper bows before the sublimity of her vision, but it is her contention that this radiance permeates the whole order of things— and the devotee stands before the altar as witness to that faith.

Running as counterpoint to the floods of light is the impoverished state of the worshipper. It is exactly in terms of inner completion, the potential to experience and feel— that the poet has been deprived. "Seeds withered unsown" —and offerings of this kind are the ones appropriate to a "Golden Divinity." Too insensitive to be aware of this fact, the other worshippers kneeling here offer only material objects—

> . . . what a few spare pence
> Have cheaply bought, to fling from hence
> In idly-asked petition.

As the last statement implies, they not only bring the wrong kind of offering, they also ask the wrong questions of Deity. Their requests for the advancement of personal projects are out of place in the supernal atmosphere of the secluded shrine. Knowing this the poet proposes that she will devote herself wholly to the service of the Divinity. In this instance, devotion is meant in its most literal sense: what the poet promises to do is to sacrifice her life to the godhead, but there is also an implication that this service will be a means of renewal.

At this point, there is a break in the thought of the poem if we imagine that the poet is worshipping a deified beauty or some unnamed goddess of the moon. But close reading of her first volume of poems does not permit this interpretation. There is nothing in the poems to equate godhead with beauty. This is, it would seem, the principle we have in common with it, while the moon, a close-circling visitor in the sky, is a convenient *tabula rasa* on which to project the Divine.[6] No more extended meaning was proposed for these things. What was central was the ideal order and beauty this deity represents, the true objects of the poet's worship and sacrifice, as many of the poems here attest.

The sense of Divinity which this poem contains was expressed more effectively in poems written later in an Imagist mode. But this element in Miss Lowell's poetry has seldom been recognized by her admirers and not at all by her detractors. It is the penalty paid for the indefiniteness of her conceptions. However, what is imprecise is not necessarily useless, and this is true of her delicate impressions of the forms of nature. To see into the corporeal forms was one of her most earnest desires and explains the images of water, light, and celestial bodies which abound in her early poems—all of these being considered as points of entry into the Infinite. In "Loon Point," to give only one example, this thought becomes explicit in an image of moonlight running through the crystalline waters of a lake to imprint unreadable secrets on the sandy bottom (*CP*, 7). That the secrets *are* unreadable does not perturb or discourage her. Her gaze shifts to other scenes and we find her, years later, returning to the same kind of setting in her account of the last moments of the Chinese poet, Li Po:

. . . You found something in the wine,
I imagine,
Since you could not leave it,
Even when, after years of wandering,
You sat in the boat with one sail,
Traveling down the zigzag rivers
On your way back to Court.

You had a dream
I conjecture.
You saw something under the willow-lights of
   the water
Which swept you to dizziness,
So that you toppled over the edge of the boat,
And gasped, and became your dream . . .

They erected a temple to you:
Great Doctor,
Prince of Poetry,
Immortal man who loved drink."
I detest wine,
And I have no desire for the temple . . .
But I would sacrifice even sobriety
If, when I was thoroughly drunk,
I could see what you saw
Under the willow-clouded water,
The day you died.

                                          [*CP*, 209]

     The interest of this poem consists in its clear-cut state-
ment of Miss Lowell's mystical attitude and her subordina-
tion of other concerns to the discovery of truth. Her subject
here is the legendary death by drowning of Li Po, a poet
with whom Miss Lowell felt a strong affinity. We notice
first the great seriousness with which she treats her story
that Li Po glimpsed an image of the Divine under the
surface of the unevenly lighted water. She does not doubt
this was possible; it is described here as the climax of his

and the direct cause of death. For herself, she says, it is an experience for which she would pay any price. At the same time, it is not something to which a precise meaning can be attached. There is no effort here even to guess the import of his vision. And this fact relates to her conception of Li Po as a "dream" which he entered fully at the moment of his death. It remains only to point out the colloquial ease with which this poem is written. One of a great mass on Oriental subjects which opened her book, *Pictures of the Floating World*, it has apparently been easy to overlook its significance and the connection it has with the attitudes expressed in her earliest work.

III

Unless all existence is a medium of revelation, no particular revelation is possible.

WILLIAM TEMPLE

In this transcendental framework it was inevitable that nature would be revalued, and there are signs of this in Miss Lowell's first book of poems. Only a short time after its appearance, the poet encountered John Gould Fletcher in London and expressed great interest in that poet's *Irradiations* and his theory of the "unrelated method" on which his poems were based. Such a response was natural on her part. The method pleased her because its essentials already existed in her own work. What Fletcher had boldly conceived was the transfer of interest in a poem from a human center to objects in the external world—not what they are to us but such meaning and value as they possess in themselves.

This may be viewed as an advance over the doctrine of Baudelaire, made famous in his sonnet, "Correspondences." In this poem nature speaks in its own voice but it is im-

plied that it exists for the benefit of man. In Fletcher and
Amy Lowell nature is represented as we actually experience
it about us: an autonomous creation that existed before man,
pays him no heed, and may survive his term on earth.
Nature, these poets would say, is not wood for our fireplaces or a source of instruction for the moral life of man,
as Ralph Waldo Emerson would have it, but what it is in
itself.

The conception can be illustrated by reference to "A
Japanese Wood-carving," a poem written by Miss Lowell
some time before meeting Fletcher. In this unusual poem,
whose form echoes the blank verse meditations of Coleridge,
the poet assumes the identity of a tree in tracing its life
through the change of the seasons and its experience of
storms and of "broad sunlit days." The poem is more effective than one might imagine. Though we balk at the attri-
bution of emotions to a tree, the lines do force a new awareness of trees, as they exist in themselves and as parts of a
divine or numinous landscape.

That she saw the tree in this way is shown by the treatment of a marine view which follows in the same poem, the
wood of the cherry tree concerned having been carved to
depict a dramatic seascape. This scene of heaving waters
and glaring light presided over by two white birds, her
"spirits of the sky" which "swoop, and soar, and scream
for very joy" is actuated by a preternatural energy, what
Emerson called "ecstasy" or "excess of life"; and the poet
soon tells us this "untamed" quality is its value for her.
The seascape brings to the quiet, firelit room where she
sits another image of transcendence by which to know the
Divine worshipped in the opening poem of the book.

However, it is not only in nature that we discover the
Numinous. We find it also in the qualities of human beings.
For most persons in the age of science this divinity is
barely noticed, but for the poet it was a truth as manifest
as the sun and equally warming. We see this if we examine
the ardent love poem on page fifty of *A Dome*. Here tone,
language, and the attitude of the devotee are very similar

to those in "Before The Altar." Instead of a votary, the poet is now a priest worshipping the beloved as one would kneel "before a holy shrine," while the "incense" of garden-flowers serves to "sanctify and bless our night of love."[7] If the skeptical choose to see in this language a veil for sexual feeling, they may turn to the poems of friendship here which show her attitude most truly or to the tributes to Mrs. Russell and Eleonora Duse written many years later. In one of these, a stanza from her "Twenty-Four Hokku on a Modern Theme," in which she celebrates Mrs. Russell—"A cloud of lilies/Or else you walk before me./Who could see clearly?"—the poet achieves a rare condensation, suggesting both the unearthliness of nature in the lilies and that of the human spirit through her fusion of the two in a single glowing image.

In these same three lines the poet suggests that we "see clearly" in nothing—and in "Hero-Worship" and other early poems we learn that her expectations of human excellence generally turn out to be ill-founded. But this does not alter her faith in an ideal purpose in life, which she expresses in "The Lamp of Life" (*CP*, 16); and she maintains it even in the face of apparent cosmic indifference to man, which is the theme of an eloquent poem in which she disallows, for herself, the comforts of Christian belief ("To Elizabeth Ward Perkins," *CP*, 13).

Both of these themes, the sense of man's loneliness and the countervailing belief in ideal purpose are expressed in what must be considered Miss Lowell's most mysterious and mystical utterance, "The Promise of the Morning Star." In studying this poem we must assume that the experiences involved were real for the poet, and that they represent an important statement of her attitudes toward the world.

Thou father of the children of my brain
By thee engendered in my willing heart,
How can I thank thee for this gift of art
Poured out so lavishly and not in vain.

What thou created never more can die,
Thy fructifying power lives in me
And I conceive, knowing it is by thee,
Dear other parent of my poetry!

For I was but a shadow with a name,
Perhaps by now the very name's forgot;
So strange is Fate that it has been my lot
To learn through thee the presence of that aim

Which evermore must guide me. All unknown,
By me unguessed, by thee not even dreamed,
A tree has blossomed in a night that seemed
Of stubborn, barren wood. For thou hast sown

This seed of beauty in a ground of truth.
Humbly I dedicate myself, and yet
I tremble with a sudden fear to set
New music ringing through my fading youth.

                                              [*CP*, 13]

   The poem is the more impressive because of the struggle
the novice poet is waging with her art: the obvious faltering
in the meter, as in line five, the muffled tone throughout,
and occasional triteness of expression, as in line seventeen.
As she tells us in stanza four, this is the work of a beginner
overcome with astonishment that she has become a poet
so suddenly, so unexpectedly, and so late: "A tree has blossomed in a night that seemed/Of stubborn, barren wood."
That she also saw this poem as filling a part in a definite
sequence of thought is shown by the place she gave it in
her volume. It appears near the end of the long section
of "lyrical poems" on the heels of the poem to Mrs. Perkins,
refusing Christian belief, and immediately preceding a poem
on the French mystic, Huysmans, which treats his conver-
sion to orthodox Catholicism. Framed in this way, the
alternative she chooses is the promise of the morning star.
This promise is not specified nor does the poet make any

attempt to describe her own moment of illumination which is implied here. All that is clear is that this was an experience of a spiritual order and the effect for her was to redeem her life. That the agency involved was not an actual star is apparent from the nature of her experience of it. It is, instead, a sphere of brightness which has joined to her resulting in the "fructifying" of her poetic gift.

As this statement suggests, her manner of expression is metaphorical, and we can reach her meaning, if at all, only by study of her chosen symbols. The most important of these concerns the import of a star that shines brilliantly at dawn only to fade in a short time at the approach of daylight. Following the thought which this suggests, we note that there is a sense in which the splendor of the world is ordinarily hidden from view. It is all but disowned in the flurry of everyday activities, directed as they are at limited, practical ends. More important still in veiling our sense of it is the weight of suffering and incompletions to which human life is subject, facts which cannot be evaded but appear in a different light when set in a cosmic perspective. In this perspective, what the speaker in the poem had suffered earlier in life is of no moment compared to the joy she feels in being linked with the creative processes of the universe. What the morning star seems to promise is the existence of a transcendent beauty and order even though this may fade, like the star that announces it, before the onset of crass, daily concerns.

This is the meaning suggested by the images of the poem, but there is a deeper level as well. The latter can only be described as the sense of divine impregnation with which these clumsy, halting lines are steeped, the mystical experience which was itself the starting point of the poem. Having converse with this Power, the poet is able to create, and the poetry which results will bear the stamp of its heavenly origins.

IV

The Poet

In the account of Miss Lowell I have given in these two
chapters I tried to show that she transcended the conventional limits of her time in style of life and range of feeling.
That this was widely understood is shown by her reputation in Boston as a radical and the label of "bohemian"
which was put on her by unfriendly observers such as
Robert Frost. It should also be recalled that this feature
of her life came from elements deeply seated in her nature.
I have already referred to the recollections of Amy by her
friend, Elizabeth Ward Perkins. The most interesting passage in this memoir describes the set of mind which Mrs.
Perkins observed in Amy Lowell from the earliest years
of their acquaintance. The italics are mine:

> The sharp images of nature gathered by the poet in
> those active out-of-door days of her childhood and
> youth served her well when ill-health and unremitting
> labor chained her to the house. Even then, if she went
> into her garden thrice in a spring, *she saw with a more
> ardent attention, felt with more keenly directed emo-
> tion than the rest of us in the springs of a life-time.*
>   *Her penetrating eye was not satisfied with seeing,*
> but the society into which she was born was well
> satisfied. There existed among her neighbors, still
> in their middle years at the end of the century,
> several Bostonians who prided themselves, in spite
> of complete freedom as to time and money, that they
> had never been outside the Commonwealth of Massa-
> chusetts.
>   This self-complacent atmosphere was not one in
> which a thirst for the unattainable is fostered. Such
> hunger and such thirst suffered with one's feet on
> ancestral ground would have been considered in

fin de siécle Boston equivalent to an unhealthy appetite for the moon. *Both poems and persons are now
alive to bear witness that from these early days the
unattainable thing that is forever distant, yet possessed in the search, was Amy Lowell's desire. . . .*

The effects of this set of mind were more far-reaching
than her friend or even the poet herself probably realized.
They account for the mystical conception of race expressed
in "The Boston Athenaeum" discussed above, just as they
account for the "doubleness" she found in nature, a
vision fostered by her splendid garden but having its
origin in her own insights. The same quality explains
the excitement which others felt in her presence as well
as her ability to inspire them to transcend their usual selves.

Key terms which appear regularly in *A Dome* as tokens
of her thought are "splendor," "majesty," "glory,"
"prismed," "shimmering," and "golden." They are descriptive of her conception of the world and exist in many
variants. In relation to human beings, she compares the
voice of a friend to a solemn pealing of bells and, in a
poem of that title, she offers another friend "Frankincense
and Myrrh" as if she were a divine being. Valuations of
this kind express her depth of response and not bemuse-
ment or naivete. The order of things as we know it is de-
fective and incomplete, she says, a fact that looms large
in these poems. In "The Lamp of Life" she contrasts our
actual circumstances to the glory we see urging us on in
the pursuit of an Ideality not possible on earth (*CP*, 16).
However, this vision is so dazzling that it dwarfs our other
concerns. It is the Numinous or Divine, her experience of
which forms the subject matter of "Before The Altar" and
other such poems, her approach to which is by means of
the "second sight" which she claims for herself in the poem,
"Dreams," just as she tells us in "New York at Night" that
"sacred communing" was her purpose in working in solitude at night. This line of thought, over-simple and seemingly obvious in the retelling, is dictated by the contents

and arrangement of the poems in this volume. A revelation
so full and intimate suggests a reason that the author
always defended these poems even though she was aware
of their feebleness of expression.

There remains the possible objection that Miss Lowell
was writing in the elevated style of late Romantic verse
and that the poems are merely a conventional use of various
elements of that philosophy, without real meaning in her
life and thought. One answer to that lies in the fervent emotion she expresses in her sonnet, "The Poet," whose theme
and imagery are such that it is virtually a summary of her
book. If we relate this poem to certain statements about
the artist made in "The Boston Athenaeum," we see that
it has the merit of defining that inner self which she described as often hidden from the contemporaries of a
writer. In her poem she speaks in general terms of *the poet,*
but it is not this generic type which she describes but her
own innermost feelings and motivations:

> What instinct forces man to journey on,
> Urged by a longing blind but dominant!
> Nothing he sees can hold him, nothing daunt
> His never failing eagerness. The sun
> Setting in splendor every night has won
> His vassalage; those towers flamboyant
> Of airy cloudland palaces now haunt
> His daylight wanderings. . . .

With great intensity and conviction the poet expresses here
her sense of the insufficiency of earthly things and goals—
"Nothing he sees can hold him"—and, alternatively, her
overpowering conviction of a transcendental reality which
she images in terms of her favorite symbols of light and
heavenly splendors. A sensibility of the kind that this
vision requires exists on the frontier of consciousness,
an idea which she dramatizes in the journey motif of the
opening lines. Another effect of this state of mind is to
center life on one's relationship to the Absolute or Divine

to which all other aspects of life become secondary. Hence the need for unceasing movement and activity, the impossibility of consummation in the limited human world and the impossibility of satisfying knowledge. One resource remains, however, and this is described in the concluding portion of "The Poet." Rejecting the ordinary gratifications of human nature, she will pass her life in contemplation and the effort to possess a portion of the Divine.

> . . . Forever done
> With simple joys and quiet happiness
> He guards the vision of the sunset sky;
> Though faint with weariness he must possess
> Some fragment of the sunset's majesty;
> He spurns life's human friendships to profess
> Life's loneliness of dreaming ecstasy.
>
> [*CP*, 17]

Instead of a lack of vital subject matter in her poems, as most critics have complained, we find a preoccupation with one of the most compelling themes, what Swinburne once described as "elemental and eternal things."

Chapter Three

The Discovery of Form

Imagism and Zen

I

However much the fact may baffle the
intellectualist and utilitarian, supra-
rational experience remains the paradox
and life-blood of religion . . . as of cre-
ative art.

HUSTON SMITH

In the nine years between the appearance of her first
book in 1912 and Miss Lowell's book of Chinese translations, *Fir-Flower Tablets* in 1921, the poet was responsible
for twelve volumes of verse and prose, as well as seventy-
two essays which appeared in various periodicals and
newspapers.[1] Among these were some of the most influential literary writings of the time—essays on the appearance
of an *American* art, on the *new* poetry, on *original* sources
of literary inspiration in foreign cultures—as well as some
of the most distinctive poetry which has come down to us
from those years. In contrast to the sixty-nine short lyrics
composing *A Dome of Many-Coloured Glass,* the poems
of these years took many unusual forms, some of them
very disturbing to the conservative minded. Much of this
work, as noted above, was prolix and casual, of little more
substance than the jottings in a newspaper. But the core
of it was sound, and all of it, as published in periodicals
and books, served the useful purpose of reawakening a
poetic consciousness in America.

An achievement of this kind in such a short space of
time would have been impossible for the groping and in-
hibited poet of *A Dome.* But Miss Lowell had chosen to
"go to school" with the Imagists in England in 1913 and
1914 and she had returned home with a new key to her own
experience and the art of expressing it. The source of this
new potency is suggested in a few cryptic lines by Ezra

Pound which he printed as the preface to *A Quinzaine for this Yule*, published in London in late 1909. (The italics are mine.)

> *Beauty should never be presented explained.* It is Marvel and Wonder, and in art we should find first these doors—Marvel and Wonder—and, coming through them, a slow understanding *(slow even though it be a succession of lightning understandings and perceptions)* as of a figure in mist, that still and ever gives to each one his own right of believing, each after his own creed and fashion.
> *Always the desire to know and to understand more deeply* must precede any reception of beauty. *Without holy curiosity and awe* none can find her, and woe to that artist whose work wears its 'heart on its sleeve'.[2]

If one takes these lines as seriously as they deserve, the reader notices at once their similarity to the mysticism of Amy Lowell as we find it in her early poems. It may be objected that Pound wrote this as a twenty-four-year-old still under the influence of Romantic ideas, but except for the shift to more colloquial diction in his later pronouncements, there is no evidence that he ever abandoned these views. In the usual account of the history of the Imagist movement, writers have stressed the differences among the poets, yet the look backward across a half century provides a different perspective. If Pound and Miss Lowell seem to agree in their manner of viewing the world, it is also interesting to note that John Gould Fletcher is now seen as a mystic, while Richard Aldington appends a note to his collected poems affirming the primacy of spirit and his sense of communion with a supernatural "potency." To this list of the original Imagists, we must add H. D. whose feeling of mystical identity with nature is a mainspring of her work, according Thomas B. Swann's study of this poet.

What once seemed so obvious, a gathering of nature pho-

tographers intent on refreshment in the open air, now
reveals its uncomfortable depths and implications. But
the real nature of Imagism might have been understood
from the first if the reader had taken the words of H. D.
at their own face value. All of the early work of this poet
betrays an openness to impression which made her an un-
acknowledged clairvoyant—and unstrung her nerves as
well. This quality and its effect on her are best expressed
in a poem called "The Gift."[3]

Sleepless nights,
I remember the initiates . . .
I have heard how in rapt thought,
in vision, they speak
with another race,
more beautiful, more intense than this . . .

This I forgot last night:
You must not be blamed . . .
As a child, a flower—any flower
tore my breat—
meadow-chicory, a common grass-tip,
a leaf shadow, a flower tint
unexpected on a winter-branch . . .

I reason:
another life holds what this lacks,
a sea, unmoving, quiet—
not forcing our strength
to rise to it, beat on beat—
a stretch of sand,
no garden beyond, strangling
with its myrrh-lilies—
a hill, not set with black violets
but stones, stones, bare rocks,
dwarf-trees, twisted, no beauty
to distract—to crowd
madness upon madness.

Only a still place
and perhaps some outer horror
some hideousness to stamp beauty,
a mark—no changing it now—
on our hearts. . . .

One should note that the poet is not rejecting beauty
("a mark—no changing it now—on our hearts") but is
rebelling against the strain it imposes on our suscepti-
bilities. This kind of awareness also characterizes John
Gould Fletcher whose conception of the "unrelated
method" was based on his concern for the qualities of
physical objects whose "secret life" he hoped to transfer
to the written page. In this he had striking initial success
in his "irradiations" and "symphonies" whose lush impressionism was the very reverse of the spareness of H. D.
But whatever their differences in style and approach, it
is clear that H. D. and Fletcher shared an ecstatic response
to the world in which the unseen was the dominant element
and mystery the primary ingredient of reality.

In the preface quoted above Pound says that knowledge
and understanding are essential components of art, but
the knowledge he favors has the same indefinability as
the mysticism of Fletcher, H. D., or Amy Lowell. In other
words, the knowledge sought by the Imagists and contained
in their work was knowledge of the suprarational, not
pleasing fancies but glimmerings of the Ideal, as Fletcher
implies at the conclusion of his "Green Symphony."

Far let the timid feet of dawn fly to catch me:
I will abide in this forest of pines:
For I have unveiled naked beauty,
And the things that she whispered to me in the
    darkness,
Are buried deep in my heart.

Now let the black tops of the pine-trees break like a
    spent wave
Against the gray sky:
There are tombs and temples and altars sun-kindled
    for me.[4]

Nothing less than this afflatus could have satisfied those
fervid souls whose meetings in London in 1913 set off a
new movement in poetry. However, before one can launch
a new wave of thought, a medium of expression is necessary; in this case, the poets needed a style suited to their
vision. Fortunately, this had been evolved as early as 1908-
1909 as the result of the meetings of a group of experimental poets led by the philosopher, T. E. Hulme.[5] Ezra
Pound joined the group, called the "school of images," in
March, 1909, in the last stages of their activity and is said
to have contributed little or nothing to the development
of their theory. But he was an apt and sympathetic pupil,
eager to experiment with new ideas and forms.

Viewed against the background of Imagist theory, Pound's
little known essay quoted above yields unexpected meanings. One of the first of these is its value in mediating
between the mysticism of the poets mentioned above and
the emphasis on a "hard, dry" descriptive style in the new
poetry advocated by their teacher, Hulme. In keeping with
this desideratum, Pound repudiates romantic "slush," the
long-exhausted emotionalism in fashion since the first
years of the nineteenth century. The new poet, Pound says,
must not wear his heart on his sleeve. On the other hand,
Marvel and Wonder, crucial ingredients of romanticism,
are still to be honored, along with Beauty, somewhat worn
after a hundred years of romantic overuse. The key to his
thought would seem to be in the sentence, "Beauty
should never be presented explained." Taken together
with statements made in other writings,[6] always of this
same blurred character, it becomes apparent that beauty
is simply Pound's way of describing the element which is to
form the substance of the new poetry. It will enter through

the doors of marvel and wonder, that is, the poet's gift of heightened awareness, and it will embody itself in "a succession of lightning understandings and perceptions as of a figure in mist," the importance of the intuitions being measured by the fact that they are to shape the poet's beliefs, his faith or creed. At this point in the argument, it seems that the writer has reversed the position with which he opened his preface because something has been explained after all, at least as far as the poet's understanding is concerned.

The apparent gap in thought may be filled by reference to a note on the image which Pound wrote for *Poetry* magazine in early 1913. Here he is explicit in giving a transcendental character to these perceptions, which, he tells us, place us beyond time and space and offer the "sense of sudden growth" experienced in the presence of great art. So the element at the heart of the new poetry is in the nature of an epiphany, which may be grasped directly through insight but cannot be explained by reason.

In other words, poetry was to take a step forward. Instead of reproducing the common fund of ideas and feelings of a given time and place, it would make itself into an instrument of discovery. Such findings as it made would be expressed emblematically as images, very puzzling to some but having a curious suggestive power. An example of the Imagist boldness and the search-in-progress may be found in the sparse language of "The Pool" by H. D.

> Are you alive?
> I touch you.
> You quiver like a sea-fish.
> I cover you with my net.
> What are you—banded one?[7]

Addressing this limpid eye of water, the poet questions the nature of an object as patently alive as it is tenuous. Covering it with the net of her intuition, it spills out, but the reader has been jarred into a fresh perception of "poolness."

Not all Imagist poems would be so hobbled as this by an intractable subject matter. As suggested in the chapters that follow, Miss Lowell's poetry at its best is a notable discovery of spiritual values, often presented in a few lines of a painter's brush.

II

The Dark Mirror

The Imagist poems of H. D. and Amy Lowell, a novel development in the writings of the rationalistic West, would have been unthinkable without the stimulus of art forms imported from a civilization very different from the practical busyness of the Occident. Examples of this exotic art, chiefly in the form of the Japanese block print had been flooding Europe and America since the 1860s and were said to have influenced certain aspects of Impressionist painting in France.[8] The informal subject matter and composition of this *genre*, as well as its use of light, had been felt as a liberation by the French, but there was more than this involved in the new cultural transfusion.[9]

To begin with, a wide range of Oriental art forms had won favor in the West by the year 1910, and they carried with them the impact a special vision of life. Eagerly scanning the new designs in painting, poetry, and the plastic arts, the Westerner was imbued, half-consciously, with their philosophy. In the case of the art forms that have had the greatest effect on twentieth-century verse, the philosophy was Zen Buddhist, and it is this vision of life which contributed the most distinctive elements to Imagism. None of the Imagists adopted the Buddhist religion, some of them may have lacked direct knowledge of its teachings, but the archetypal Imagist poem, based on the Japanese *haiku*, is the product of the mode of consciousness which has been elaborated in Zen and is now exerting a far-reaching influence in the West.[10] For this reason, it is possible to see the Imagists as the first exponents of a "set of mind" which is now becoming popular fifty years after the subsidence of their movement.

This philosophy involves a radical alteration in our point of view toward the world and experience. In contrast to the attitudes that have prevailed in the West under the ancient Greek philosophers, medieval Christendom, and finally modern science, greatest dogmatist of all, Zen Buddhism suggests that we know nothing worth knowing in the human sense, and that the world we inhabit is, quite simply, a chasm of emptiness, the "Miraculus Void" out of which suddenly issue designs of incredible delicacy—an iris, a sea-shell, tree, or bird—which are almost instantly reabsorbed into Nothingness, like the frail gold tracings of a rocket against the sky. It is not only pool-ness and tree-ness that need to be explored but the whole range of created nature, which science can only inventory and dissect.

Whatever the nature of things may be, the answer has not been found in science, and the heart of the problem consists in the fact that "being" exhibits qualities which are not reducible to reason at all. No logical construct can account for our existence, and even if it were possible to imagine a common sense explanation for the appearance of life, as bits of protoplasm in some ancient sea, there remains the fact of the beauty, heroism, and spirituality characterizing life at its highest pitch.

Does this mean that no real knowledge is possible? In this situation Zen is prepared and bristling with counsel. Man is capable of understanding, it says, but not by way of the intellect, whose operations always impose a spurious simplicity on life. It follows that man must give up the thought that he can conceptualize what exists in a realm beyond reason, that is, the nature of his life and the world. Having admitted this, he can turn the powers of the deeper reaches of the mind, where the existence of Buddha-nature "not only in man but in everything animate and inanimate"[11] is the basis of insight and the guarantee of meaningful knowledge. In the language of Victor Hugo, who reached these same conclusions independently,

> It is an extraordinary thing but it is within oneself that one must look for what is without. The dark mirror is deep down in man. There is the terrible chiaroscuro. A thing reflected in the mind is more vertiginous than when seen directly. It is more than an image—it is the simulacrum, and in the simulacrum there is a specter. . . . When we lean over this well, we see there, at an abysmal depth in a narrow circle, the great world itself.[12]

We "know" the world, we do not merely sense it, because it is already within us, but in some fashion inconceivable to reason. In the same way that man is open to the world—in mysterious converse with its forms—he is a creature open to the Divine, human awareness of the Infinite coming first to the worthy in the breathless experience of *satori*, a mystical transport, but later diffusing itself into the sense of the "indescribable wonder" of things, known in Zen as "divine ordinariness."[13] What has been gained from these experiences is not knowledge in an intellectual sense but a new relationship to the world. One is no longer outside pondering experience (thinking about it) but immersed in the stream of life itself. A Western student, who had been training in Kyoto for seven years, explained once to what end Zen practices lead: "No parapsychic experiences, as far as I am aware. But you wake up in the morning and the world seems so beautiful that you can hardly stand it."[14] Opinion concerning the nature of this enlightenment, whether parapsychic or not, would depend on the viewpoint of the observer, but it is basic to Zen theory that access to the Infinite is a normal attribute of the human mind.

III

Wordless Poetry,
Painting By Not Painting

The most striking art forms to which Zen has given rise are implied in the famous Flower Sermon of Buddha. Standing on the side of a mountain, symbol of infinity, with his disciples gathered about him, the Enlightened One "simply held aloft a golden lotus" without speaking. Something momentous had occurred in his mind, and for this very reason he did not choose "to identify his discovery with any verbal expression."[15] Whether derived from this legendary act or simply the result of concurrent strains of thought, Zen artists have always sought to embody the truth and artistic philosophy implied in this gesture. Zen gardens of sand and rock, bare, undistracting rooms, poetry "which says nothing"—each of these is aimed at "a higher angle of vision" than one is likely to meet in ordinary life and in many varieties of art as well. In presenting the golden lotus as he did, Gautama was pointing to a miracle of nature—and so discovering or defining reality—at the same time that he indicated that man has no speech or logic to encompass it. (Choosing a very similar subject matter, Wordsworth held up the golden daffodil which he "explains" in accordance with a set of human meanings imposed on it.)

But this does not carry us very far into the anomaly of unformed art and speechless communication. Zen art is based first of all on moments of enhanced awareness. The flower above had inspired a special awakening—not a deliberate search for a subject, but a sudden illumination carrying with it the sense of a "timeless moment" (Watts, 181). The result of this is definition in a special sense. Something essential has been glimpsed and is detached from the object or the scene to form the image in the art.

What makes this possible is the "echo chamber" of the

human mind. As noted above, Buddhist thought envisages a continuum between nature and the human mind, one aspect of which is the great "store-consciousness" in man. This reservoir, supra-individual in character, contains "the seeds of all possible forms," of which it is, in a sense, the résumé. Accordingly, the recognition which comes with the artist's insight will reach beyond logical formulation to disclose the object itself, or its "pure suchness," as this is known in Japan. It is clear then that the distinction of Zen consists in the discarding of general ideas, which can only *abstract*, to offer an image of "the-thing-in-itself," the face which the object would present to eternity. An art of this kind, centered in mystical awareness, can only be as good as the intuition of the artist, and it requires for its fulfillment a corresponding rarity of thought in its audience (Watts, 75 and 180).

This is the more true of Zen because of. its panting desire for the Absolute. Few forms of art show so consistent a regard for "final questions," although it excludes the treatment of them in terms of logical propositions. What is most striking on the surface of Zen art, as in the gardens and austere interiors mentioned above, is the elimination of all that is accidental or superficial to reveal the essences of things. And so we have, in addition to the objects themselves, in their pure suchness, a representation of the "Void" or silence which surrounds them and out of which they suddenly issue. This element of Zen art is more than a reference to origins or a statement of man's most fundamental relationship. In Buddhist thought we are concerned to know the objects of nature because each form *is* the "Void," not in the usual pantheistic sense, but more directly still, as the sudden materialization of the Eternal, a thrusting of the hand through the veil (Watts, 75).

Among the forms of Zen art which embody this vision, the most striking, perhaps, is a style of painting known as *sumi-e*. This curious and eloquent art consists of brush-strokes of black ink set against a large expanse of empty space which serves a symbolic purpose. Though this is a religious art, its subject matter is taken from the objects of nature, and the achievement of the artists consists not only in the vivid realization of these forms, but their power to evoke the divine, the blank space surrounding their designs suggesting the Miraculous Void to which the objects of nature are "integrally related" (Watts, 179). This power to bring the Void to life and to relate life to the Void is suggested in the following passage by Dorothy Van Ghent in which she notes a resemblance between the supernaturalism of *Wuthering Heights* and the spirit found in the Chinese landscape paintings:

> The attitude toward life in *Wuthering Heights* is rather one of awed contemplation of an unregenerate universe than a feeling for values and dis-values in types of human intercourse. It is an attitude that is expressed in some of the great Chinese paintings of the Middle Ages, where the fall of a torrent from an enormous height, or a single huge wave breaking under the moon, or a barely indicated chain of mountains lost among mists, seems to be animated by some mysterious, universal, half-divine life which can only be "recognized," not understood.[16]

All of the considerations above, including the extra-personal character which Miss Van Ghent detects in *sumi-e*, apply equally to the form of Japanese poetry known as the *haiki*. This form, perfected by the Zen monk, Basho, is also concerned with the life, shapes, and moods of nature, its peculiarity consisting in the fact that it is limited to a total of seventeen syllables. The resulting compression serves the same purpose as the spareness of detail in *sumi-e*. What is squeezed out is the usual effort to editorialize plants, seas, and mountains, to explain or to conceptualize such phenomena, and what is left is the germ of "the-thing-in-itself" in the form of a visual image.

For this purpose, it might seem that words would be a poor substitute for painting, but this is not the case. In the *haiku* the poet presents a nature image as defined in the mind, and the abstractness of language allows the poet to manipulate the subject and limit himself to significant detail. These become the purveyors of his insight, and in these poems they are joined to an expression of mood which poetry can convey more directly and exactly than painting. This element in the *haiku*, emphasized by Basho, is the means to express the correspondence between human sensibility and the various aspects of nature, a part of the Buddhist conception of the interpenetration of all phenomena. In this way man enters the spirit of nature, and this same faculty gives him an awareness of the divine, which is suggested by the silence surrounding the sparse phrases.

All three of these qualities of the *haiku*—its effectiveness as visual image, its expression of the unity between man and nature, and its suggestion of the divine—are present in Amy Lowell's "Twenty-Four Hokku On A Modern Theme" from which the following are taken.

1.
Again the larkspur,
Heavenly blue in my garden.
They, at least, unchanged.

5.
In the ghostly dawn
I write new words for your ears—
Even now you sleep.

13.
Watching the iris,
The faint and fragile petals—
How am I worthy?

24.
Staying in my room,
I thought of the new spring leaves.
That day was happy.

[*CP*, 441-42]

The reader can gain no proper notion of this poem from
disconnected fragments, but the examples chosen illustrate
the qualities of the form in a way not matched by un-
satisfactory translations from the Japanese. What we have
is a rare compression of statement, but the substance consists in halftones and suggestions not well suited to critical analysis. As Alan Watts points out in his book, *The
Way of Zen*, the *haiku* is a form which calls on the reader
to complete its statement. It is "a pebble thrown into the
pool of the listener's mind, evoking associations out of
the richness of his own memory."

IV

*What has found expression in painting as
Impressionism will soon find expression in
poetry as free verse.*

T. E. HULME, 1908

I have included this account of Zen to give an external
frame of reference for the poetry of the Imagists and that
of Amy Lowell in particular. My first aim has been to
identify a legitimate subject matter for this poetry since
Imagism has been widely misunderstood as a type of
poetry which deals only with the external appearance of
things and fails therefore to interpret human experiences.
How false this is to the real nature of Imagism may be
gauged by the account given above of its antecedents in
Buddhist ideas. The poets gathered in London in 1910
were seeking a new mode of apprehending reality which
would do justice to their experience without reliance on
discarded beliefs. In essence, this is the situation set forth
in the poems and essays of Wallace Stevens who seeks new
principles to nourish life because, in his view, all the old
beliefs are dead and "the heaven of Europe is empty."[17]
This kind of agnosticism was commonplace among the

intellectuals born in the last third of the nineteenth century. Its causes may be traced in part to the discoveries of an aggressive and materialistic science, which by 1900— when Stevens was twenty-one and Miss Lowell twenty-six —had destroyed the basis for age-old systems of belief, or so it seemed at the time; and the poets had been quick to take account of the new knowledge. Of the many outstanding figures who emerged in the poetic renaissance of 1912-1922, nearly all were at one with Amy Lowell in questioning and rejecting inherited social and religious beliefs. But this is not to say that they were prepared to disallow their own experience in favor of scientific theories which lead to a mechanical and soulless universe.

The same breakdown of belief had occurred somewhat earlier in Europe as the result of the "worship of Reason" institutionalized by the French Revolution. There it was an important factor in giving rise to the Impressionist movement which Arnold Hauser has defined as the prevailing style in European thought and art at least until 1910.[18] This style consists in the seizing on the immediate *impression*, the effect in the mind of a concrete experience, as the basis for our knowledge or estimation of the world. The revolutionary element in this process, which produced intense hostility at the time, consists in the fact that it is a direct apprehension of the world, without regard to previously established and socially approved formulas, rules, or ideas—and so abandons the mediating role of reason in much the same way and for similar reasons that this happens in Zen.

In its most famous expression, the French painting of the late nineteenth century, it is seen as the effort to reproduce the interplay of different colors and intensities of light as these are affected by the atmosphere surrounding a given subject or scene. In a sense this is true, for light becomes the absolute in Impressionist painting and all material forms take their cue from that, being revealed, dissolved, or translated as it changes in character. Because of this dematerialization of vision and the ethereal effects

we often find in these painters, some persons have been
led to see a mystical or "semireligious" impulse at work.
In his book, *Rococo to Cubism*, Wylie Sypher discusses
this aspect of Impressionism and points out that it is
analogous to the scientific discoveries of that day which
were beginning to reduce the world to a single "impon-
derable substance" in which matter and energy are fused.[19]
In any case it is difficult to overlook what Sypher has
called "the special temper of light" in these paintings, or
the fact that their subjects, for all their impermanency
as objects of nature, have "a presence that is also eternal."[20]
Sypher treats these matters at some length, but the halo
effect and the unearthly coloring must be apparent to all
viewers in some of the best work by Monet and Bonnard,
to cite only two of these painters. At a time when the
dogmas of religion had lost much of their authority, the
ordinary artist recovered the Numinous in a mysterious
light that was seen to be adherent to almost any object
when it was closely observed.

Retiring to Giverny in 1883, Monet rearranged the course
of the River Epté so that it flowed through his garden
forming a large pool planted with water lilies and bordered
by wisteria and willow trees. There, in the latter part of
his long life (1840-1926), he gave himself to a final vision
inspired by

> his profound feeling for a world in movement, a cosmic
> reality in which the miraculous and enchanting are
> more real than nature itself . . . Reflection, the mere
> suggestion of the object that renders it far more seduc-
> tive than reality itself, and the resultant disem-
> bodiment of the concrete world surrounding us—
> these were Monet's contributions to painting.[21]

In this special world where "frail forms" come and go in
"an envelope of light"[22] and the essential quality of
things consists in their inexplicable character, we are
back once more to the vision of Zen of which Impres-

sionism may be seen as a close relative and Imagism a direct descendant.

Against this background of the Oriental antecedents of Imagism and the impressionist movement of which it formed a part, it should be possible to detach what is distinctive in Imagist poetry. This might be expressed as the movement into "the unsyllabled sea," a phrase used by Emily Dickinson in a poem that points to the unknowableness of life but concludes with an affirmation of the rapture of intuitive awareness.

It was, however, chiefly the puzzlements of life which came to T. E Hulme, the young English founder of Imagism who perished in the first World War. Hulme recognized that his age required a new method for poetry and he sensed the direction it should take, but he himself was unsuccessful in translating his vision into poetry. That vision seemed to consist primarily of a fresh awareness of the interaction between the human spirit and the suprarational which surrounds us, the "unsyllabled sea," in Miss Dickinson's language. The sense that the various features of the world exist not as discrete objects but in positive relationship to us is a very old one, but it was given a new importance by Hulme, who was preoccupied by the nonlogical core of our experience.

His own effort to penetrate this area first shows itself in his account, quoted by Sir Herbert Read, of his travels in Canada in 1906. Writing to a friend, he observed, "I have got lots of ideas and experience and am very glad I came, even if it were only for a suitable image I thought of one day, working in the railway, for what I was talking to you about just before I left London." To this Sir Herbert adds a passage extracted from a lecture Hulme gave two years later: "Speaking of personal matters, the first time I felt the necessity or inevitableness of verse, was in the peculiar quality of feeling which is induced by the flat spaces and wide horizons of the virgin prairie of western Canada."[23]

Three things seem especially significant here: (1) the strong emphasis Hulme gives to experience once viewed as peripheral at best—that is, the realization of the-thing-in-itself, the suchness of an object in the phrase used by the Japanese; (2) the choice of the image instead of description to render it; and (3) the recognition of poetry as the medium required to shape and contain these discoveries. That Hulme was aware that he was proposing a new view of meaning, at least in terms of the traditional content of poetry, is indicated in his statement, "The fallacy that language is logical, or that meaning is. *Phrases have meaning for no reason.*" Applied to the writing of poetry, this principle results in the following prescription for the creation of a poem:

> Think of sitting at that window in Chelsea and seeing the chimneys and lights in the dusk. And then, imagine that by contemplation this will transfer itself bodily on to paper.[24]

It is difficult to imagine a subject less apt to please the Victorian tastes of Hulme's time, or even the conservatives of today. Such persons would consider the subject better suited to painting than to an art they respected for the lessons it has to teach. The element of "human interest" has been excluded here in the ordinary sense of an appeal to man's social instincts, and what is worse, reasoning itself has been short-circuited. The contemplation that Hulme mentions is not a ratiocinative process but a mystical absorption which results in the reconstitution of these chimneys and lights in the dusk in the shape of the artist's intuition.[25]

Hulme's radical program for poetry, differing from any that had gone before, was the result of close studies of modern French poetry and thought which he made on his return from Canada. Also, at this same time (1907), he became familiar with the Japanese *haiku* and its philosophy, which was soon to be widely admired and imitated in France. Armed with a new vision and understanding, Hulme returned to London to propound his ideas to a group of followers in the "School of Images" of 1908-1909.

At the center of Hulme's thought was his awareness that there has been an alteration in human consciousness. This alteration consists in a shift from an inner life structured by socially defined attitudes, such as we find in the epics of Homer, the romances of the Middle Ages and the moralized narratives of Tennyson, to an inner life that has been liberated for individual response and perception. The importance of the shift, for good and ill, can hardly be overestimated since it means that man is given access, for the first time, to his own selfhood, instead of the uniform and bland-featured masks which society had always imposed.

In the realm of art it has produced a transfer of interest from the deeds of the hero, as in the ballad and epic and the large public theme (both of these being seen as the misleading abstractions of society), to the truths of the individual awareness. As the result of this change, "the mystery of things," says Hulme, once sought in action, has now come to be found in "introspection," which he denominates as "the momentary phases of the poet's mind."[26] This new form of expression, intended to reproduce the contours of a thought, must have a freedom superior to the modes of the past, that is, the free verse that was developed in France in the 1880s and popularized in English by the Imagists who followed Hulme.

At this point it is essential to recall that the analysis of Hulme was made well before the facts. No such thing as Imagist verse existed at the time that Hulme was developing his theory (1906-1909), and in retrospect it can be seen that his insights were essential to the creation of this new voice for poetry. Chief among his sources of inspiration was the practice of the French Impressionist painters. "What has found expression in painting as Impressionism will soon find expression in poetry as free verse," he said, and the admiration he had for these painters must have encouraged him to adopt the image as the means to express the new vision in poetry. If poetry was to advance, he believed, it must do so with the Impressionists' disregard for story and literal appearance and their seizure on the "spirit" of scenes.[27] This purpose underlies Hulme's concern with nonliterary subjects for verse: the lights and chimneys seen through his window, the flattened spaces of an endless prairie. Hulme felt deeply the meaningfulness of experiences which defy logical ordering. Meanings of this sort can be evoked only by image and what results will be just such a reinventory of the world that the agnostic poets of his time were seeking.

That Hulme aimed at such a reordering of belief, a new world-view, is confirmed by Sir Herbert Read and clearly suggested in another note for a poem, this time to express the Numinous (*"force majeure"*) which is "a thing of terror beyond us" as well as something built inside human nature. In this passage it is also interesting to note the related insistence on revelation of the-thing-on-itself:

> Dome of Brompton in the mist, transfer that to art . . . everything for art is a thing in itself, and the words moved until they became a dome, a solid, separate world, a dome seen in mist, a thing of terror beyond us, and not of us. A definite *force majeure* (all the foundations of the scaffolding are in us, but we want an illusion, falsifying us, something independent of foundations). A long pillar.[28]

For this view of the mystery enfolding life, along with the demand that poetry serve as a reflecting mirror, it is evident that the Orient could offer much instruction. According to F. S. Flint, one of the participants, the poets of Hulme's group experimented with many models in the effort to create a poetry "akin in spirit to the Japanese."[29] But the form finally adopted, in the accepted prototypes written by Hulme and Pound, was a variant of the *haiku*, somewhat loosened in form but showing all the other essential qualities of this poetry. This can be seen in a wellknown poem Hulme wrote in 1908, perhaps the first Imagist poem to appear in print.

Autumn

A touch of cold in the autumn night,
I walked abroad
And saw the ruddy moon lean over a hedge,
Like a red-faced farmer.
I did not stop to speak but nodded,
And round about were the wistful stars
With white faces like town children.[30]

In terms of literary form, we note that the poem has the concision, objectivity, and suggestiveness of its Oriental models. And we also notice that Hulme has adopted the mystical overtones of Japanese poetry. Although the poem is seemingly casual, the experience of the stroller is with a set of celestial bodies and what it asserts is a close human connection with them. In this respect, the choice of subject is perfectly consistent with the ideas of Hulme reviewed above and the purpose of his theory and experimentation could be stated as follows: to lift the content of poetry to the realm of extra-logical meaning, using the pictorial method of Impressionism and to the end that the poet achieves a new relationship to reality.

V

The image is itself the speech.

EZRA POUND

In the best work of its leading exponents, Imagism shows itself as a composite of many origins, chiefly Symbolist, Impressionist, Oriental, and even Greek. In these pages I intended to show the centrality of the Oriental contribution. Certain features of Impressionist painting, as noted above, have also been traced to Japanese art, but in Imagism the impact was more far-reaching.

This influence consisted first of all in a new point of view, as this was embodied in the *haiku* and other forms of art with which the Imagists were familiar. In contrast to the rational and materialistic outlook of the West, Buddhist art and thought are solidly fixed in a concern with the eternal. This fascination with Essence, which reduced Zen gardens to sand and rock and poems to bare, single images provided a new focus for the Occidental, somewhere on Emily Dickinson's "unsyllabled sea." Although poems of this kind seem meaningless to some readers, the new interest in the suprarational was a move to the center of reality away from the inadequate abstractions of reason and science.

Having reached this new vantage point, it was necessary for the poets to have a new subject and this was provided by the special view of nature found in the Japanese art and writing we have discussed. The Absolute, which is their real subject, cannot be approached directly but the artist can occupy himself with the part of it which thrusts itself into the visible world. In other words, he can deal with the suchness of things as they stream endlessly from the Great Void, nature in itself, as we found it treated in Amy Lowell's poem, "The Japanese Wood-Carving."

Nevertheless, the new subject and new angle of vision could not in themselves produce an interpretation of any value. For this the poet was obliged to call on the resources of the so-called store-consciousness, the power of the mind to decipher the world in terms of human correspondences. Because they are extralogical these intuitions cannot be expressed in rational propositions. Their expression requires another language and this was provided by the unqualified image of Zen. In this way, a new form was provided as well as the new subject and point of view. The poem would consist primarily of an image with little or no explanation inasmuch as "The image is itself the speech" in the words of Ezra Pound. This imagistic structure would serve as the organizing center for other elements in the poetry, such as the ironic attitudes taken from French Symbolism and such elements of narrative and logical statement as are necessary to interpret the poet's intuition—to throw bridges from him to the common sense world.[31]

The effect of the practice of these principles has been the appearance of a kind of poetry as painting. In the view of some critics this poetry is cold and unemotional but the complaint is belied by the effect of the poems on their readers. In the best of them there is a special intensity of feeling called forth by the new freedom for individual response.

Most of the qualities described here may be seen in "The Camellia Tree of Matsue," a highly colored visionary poem by Amy Lowell whose theme is unmistakable even though exact interpretation may be difficult. The setting is Japanese, and it is taken from a group of "Lacquer Prints" which she wrote to reproduce the quality of the *haiku.*

> At Matsue,
> There was a Camellia Tree of great beauty
> Whose blossoms were white as honey wax
> Splashed and streaked with the pink of fair coral.
> At night,
> When the moon rose in the sky,
> The Camellia Tree would leave its place
> By the gateway,
> And wander up and down the garden,
> Trailing its roots behind it
> Like a train of rustling silk.
> The people in the house,
> Hearing the scrape of them upon the gravel,
> Looked out into the garden
> And saw the tree,
> With its flowers erect and peering,
> Pressed against the shoji.
> Many nights the tree walked about the garden,
> Until the women and children
> Became frightened,

And the Master of the house
Ordered that it be cut down.
But when the gardener brought his axe
And struck at the trunk of the tree,
There spouted forth a stream of dark blood;
And when the stump was torn up,
The hole quivered like an open wound.

[*CP*, 205]

The impact of this poem is gained by a series of short, direct statements which present not only the appearance of the flowering tree but also a sequence of clearly defined actions. Although these are fantastic, there is no suggestion that any explanation is due or necessary and the effect is much like that of the sober rehearsal of a fairy tale, which very likely inspired it. However, it is not magic which concerns the poet but an uncanny insight into nature.

This insight might be described as the discovery of sentience where the timid would prefer not to find it. If man looks out at nature, there is another sense in which nature looks back at him. Hence the spectral atmosphere of the poem which suggests the strangeness we find as soon as we look closely at the forms of nature. The poet accomplishes this in the first few lines by pointing to the singular beauty of the camellia. In a universe controlled by mechanistic laws and the strictures of reason this radiance would be as impossible as the actions ascribed to the tree, so the understanding covertly established with the reader holds that if the one is impossible, so is the other, leaving us with the uneasy alternative of groping among transcendental mysteries.

But this notion does not exhaust the content of the poem. Miss Lowell has written an affirmation not a statement of confusion. Underlying the fable is the theme of unity of being and the coextensiveness of mind and matter. In a world whose primary quality is design, each atom achieving identity through complex interlinkings, mind and sentience are also found to be primary—as in the "gaze" of the flower at the human face *which alone is capable of apprehending its beauty and so realizing for it* its flower-nature. It is this quality of interpenetration and sentiency to which the poem is addressed. If the ground quivers when the Camellia is torn out, it is because the tissue of being is broken and the dark blood that spouts from the severed trunk seems appropriate to an object whose blossoms scan their surroundings with such eager intent.

It remains now to indicate the Oriental elements found in this poem as a means to understand Miss Lowell's Imagist mode. First, it is clear that structure and tone have been determined by Miss Lowell's Japanese models. The body of the poem consists of a single image, and this is the carrier of the meaning of the poem. "The image is itself the speech," and the subject chosen is the classic one of nature as it appears to the impersonal gaze of the Zen Buddhist.

The resulting objectivity sets the tone for the poem. The lines are not lacking in emotion but the poet's feeling is contained by the insight concerned and not emotions of a personal kind. As suggested above, the austerity is the result of the insistence on Essence, a habit of mind that minimizes personal reactions and leads to the singleness of effect found in her Japanese models.

But the emphasis on compressed imagistic statement could not of itself produce the vivid pictorialism we find in "The Camellia Tree of Matsue." This was chiefly inspired by the affinities which Miss Lowell felt for the Japanese color print, her earliest artistic enthusiasm. At its best, in the great landscapes of Hokusai and Hiroshige, this genre produced studies of nature which were steeped in Buddhist awareness, and at the same time were models of arresting and clear-cut design. The art consisted in the isolation of a few expressive motifs, such as an ocean wave or the slopes Fujiyama, and the highly colored presentation of these in some unusual perspective which bared their meaning. A mannered rather than a realistic art, its chief emphasis was on "the line of analysis" representing the artist's insight into the nature of his subject.

What the American poet gained from this model can be seen in "The Camellia Tree," whose effectiveness depends on the selection of a few significant details rendered in the brilliant colors and sharp "cut edges" of the Japanese print. That Miss Lowell had a special gift for this kind of word-painting can hardly be doubted. It was her trademark from the time of the appearance of her first Imagist verses and is the chief distinquishing feature of her work.

We are prepared now to account for Amy Lowell's rise to fame at a time of life when most poets have long since passed their prime. Regardless of the worldly, practical side of the Bostonian (which was very conspicuous to her contemporaries), Miss Lowell was essentially a contemplative and visionary. This was the innermost core of her being, influenced to a great extent by her lifelong interest in the Orient.[33] She had announced her concern with Eternality in the two epigraphs chosen for her first book and it determines the content for the larger number of poems she chose for that volume. Unfortunately, the idiom and forms of the Romantic poets whom she imitated at this stage were incapable of translating her vision. In effect, it reduced her to abstract statement and generalization about her experiences which left the reader unmoved and unconvinced. The core of her awareness, though dimly suggested, could find no adequate voice. This was provided by the mingled currents of Oriental and European art offered to her as models by the Imagists in London. Given the possibilities she found in their techniques, she need not depend on description. She could present the substance of the experience itself.

In this way, Miss Lowell's gift for the exact sensory detail could be exploited and above all the faculty of intuitive apprehension. The light by which we see the Camellia Tree is a ghostly one because it is the inner vision described by Victor Hugo and endorsed by Pound in his preface of 1909. Though the effect of Hulme's teachings was often to stress the physical appearance of things as clues to reality, Pound, as we have learned, stressed the primacy of inner vision and its mystical and transcendental character. Pound's treatment of these matters, though little noticed, was an important addition or clarification of Imagist theory. No doubt the substance of these views was passed along to Amy Lowell when she was his "pupil" in London. In any case, this piece of writing defines the real meaning of Imagism for her poetry. Having adopted this mode she could return with new force to the subjects treated in her first book. Though seldom recognized as such by critics or readers, the numinous landscape or object now became the feature of her work which brought her widespread attention and admiration. It was known most commonly as her "vividness" of presentation, a quality which sometimes appeared momentarily in her long works as well as in the brief, widely known impressionistic pieces.

Chapter Four

Explorations

Middle Years: 1913-1921

I

Conquests

After her adoption of Imagist practices in 1913, the poetry of Amy Lowell centered in the treatment of the numinous scene or object with increasing refinement and flexibility. It was not, of course, her only interest, nor could it ever be a formula for writing poetry. Had this been true, Miss Lowell would have been reduced, like Wallace Stevens in the latter part of his career, to the writing of illustrations for a set of reasoned positions subject to the limitations of abstract thought. But the very opposite was true. As we see in her critical essays, systematic thought was uncongenial to Amy Lowell's mind and so she saw the more deeply. Her mind, absorbed by some impression of interest to her, an object, a person, a scene in a garden, would be suddenly illuminated so that its hidden nature was disclosed. But the process has nothing to do with reasoning in the usual sense, nor was the poet always aware of the meaning of her intuitions. Nevertheless, knowledge gained in this way has always been our most satisfactory guide to the world around us.

In an essay he wrote on Emily Dickinson, Richard Wilbur remarked: "For such a sensibility, it was natural and necessary that things be touched with infinity."[1] It was natural and necessary because Miss Dickinson sensed the infinite without and within herself, as Amy Lowell seemed to do in these brief, airy verses she once wrote about the beloved one:

Prime
Your voice is like bells over roofs at dawn
When a bird flies
And the sky changes to a fresher color.
Speak, speak, Beloved.
Say little things

For my ears to catch
And run with them to my heart.

[*CP*, 444]

The achievement of the poem consists in implanting an idea while appearing to be nothing more than a lightly done water color. At first we are affected by an unforgetable image of daybreak; then we notice that the qualities of the scene have been transferred to the Beloved. In brief, she has been set in the perspective of infinity through the use of analogy and a few sparse details. This is the infiniteness that Amy Lowell always found in human nature, and her insistence on it may be taken as the starting point for the other great theme of her work.

To borrow language again from Wilbur's essay on Dickinson, Miss Lowell was one who never let us forget that she was subject to tragic deprivations in her emotional life. Though this is true, it is not enough to say that the denial was a mockery of her imperious nature. The injury was still more deep-seated. Miss Lowell felt that she had been deprived of her inmost identity—that she had been separated from herself. The result of this is the theme of revolt against social constraints, which is the chief outward feature of her poetry. At first glance this would appear to have no relation to her impressionism as described above. But in terms of her own frame of thought, this theme can be seen to merge with the other of the numinous object. In her treatment both of the world of nature and the human individual, the poet directs our attention to the primacy of spirit and the necessity to respect it—though as a Lowell she was mindful of the claims of society and willing to honor them. In Miss Lowell's case this divided allegiance created an impasse in her personal life and she released the venom of her resentment in her poems of frustrated love, most of which should be viewed as purgatives of emotion and not as the products of a finished art.

In her personal life she achieved at least a partial solution which speaks well for the largeness of her nature. This was the attachment she formed with Mrs. Harold Russell, a widowed actress who became her companion in 1914. Endowed with rare gifts of sensitivity and tact, Mrs. Russell was credited with giving Amy Lowell "a heart," and her services to the poet in advice and literary research were of untold value. In return Amy gave unstintingly to Mrs. Russell, in every sense, and after her death this included even her home and her fortune in trust. Though the relationship could not replace the lost domain of love, it was a mating of souls which ended Miss Lowell's protracted loneliness and gave her the spirit to carry forward her career. In a sense Amy Lowell fully recognized, Mrs. Russell gave life to the books the poet produced after 1914. In consequence, Mrs. Russell bulks large among the subjects of Amy's poetry. It was a bond of love which became one of the most fully reported in literary annals, not only by the poet herself, but by all her friends who have written about her life.

In the meantime, the failure of *A Dome* in 1912 sent Miss Lowell scurrying in search of new inspiration for her wilted verse. This was provided at the end of that same year by the appearance in London of the *avant garde* Imagists, a small group of poets led by Ezra Pound. Miss Lowell arrived in England in the spring of 1913, and her personality and wealth gave her easy access to Ezra Pound, H. D., Richard Aldington, John Gould Fletcher, and F. S. Flint. Pound and his followers made special efforts to be pleasing to this august visitor, and there followed earnest conferences in which they literally rewrote her poems giving them the firmness and precision the Imagists prized (Damon, 208-209). Her meeting with Fletcher was also momentous, and a short time after hearing his unpublished *Irradiations*, Amy herself was writing impressions of unusual verve and suggestiveness. The relationships begun in this way seemed satisfactory on all sides, so it was natural that Miss Lowell should return in the summer of 1914.

The second trip marked the commencement of Mrs. Russell's duties as companion and this was staged with an eye for effect—in the maroon limousine and train of servants which attended Miss Lowell at every step and seemed to presage some change in her relationship with the others of the group. The story of Miss Lowell's break with Pound, her teacher, has been recounted many times but the facts are usually slanted in Pound's favor. In depriving this young man of the Imagist leadership, Miss Lowell was certainly guilty of the wiles of a Machiavelli. But it is relevant to note that Pound was only the adapter of the theory of Hulme. He was not in any sense the author or proprietor of Imagism, and his arbitrary and dictatorial manners had created much discontent among his followers. When Miss Lowell proposed to sponsor new volumes of their joint work with no editorship or control over the contents, they turned to this mild suzerainty with relief.

Ezra Pound, in the meantime, had joined Wyndham Lewis in a grandiose and absurd venture to renew *all of the arts*, and so the practical effect of Amy Lowell's actions was to convert Imagism from a brief episode in Pound's erratic career to a powerful movement which helped to reshape American poetry. Acting alone or with his reticent followers, Pound was incapable of the effort required to overcome the inertia and conservatism of American poetry, frozen in its insipid and moralizing Victorian forms. As for Amy Lowell, it might be said that Imagism became her hobby-horse, but a truer reading of the events would acknowledge that an incipient insurrection in the arts had found a great leader. Looking back on the history of the time as so many writers have done, it is always the personality of Amy Lowell which detaches itself as the most vivid and conspicuous element. Without her, the major figures may have performed in much the same way—but to an empty hall in a country too occupied with "business as usual" to pay serious heed to some of the most individual and exacting poets who have ever written. The great national venture of the "new poetry" from 1914 to 1925 may be said to have been Amy Lowell's part in the evolution of our artistic life.[2]

That the new poetry would be aggressive and forthright
was soon apparent. In late 1914 Miss Lowell published
Sword Blades and Poppy Seed, a volume which seemed to
echo the belligerence then erupting in Europe. An uneven
book, with many blemishes, it nonetheless contained elements of real importance for the advance of American
poetry. Among these were its novel free verse and polyphonic forms, its impressionism, and its assertion of a
radical social and sexual ethic. This was the first American
book in the new, controversial forms. It was very widely
read, and the impression it left was of a vigorous and in-
surgent experimentalism.

Some of the poets who had contributed to Miss Lowell's
new perspective were celebrated by her in *Six French Poets,*
1915. A graceful *causerie,* originally presented as lectures
before Boston society women, the essays are more in the
nature of an expression of enthusiasms than formal criticism. However, this well-circulated volume had a real
usefulness. It was the only up-to-date source from which
Americans might gain knowledge of the most recent trends
in French poetry at a time when they were seeking to overcome the age-old dependence on English letters and culture.

The independent and experimental attitude represented
by these volumes was also shown in the three anthologies
of Imagist verse Miss Lowell supervised in 1915, 1916, and
1917. Besides her own work, they included poetry by
Aldington, H. D., Flint, Fletcher, and D. H. Lawrence.
Sturdy, attractive, and of sound quality, the three collections were a key factor in firing the poetic fever and revolt
which swept the country by 1916. Improbable as this seems
today, poetry had become a national pastime by that date,
whole phalanxes of earnest souls rising suddenly and
delivering themselves of portentous free verse. *Spoon River
Anthology,* 1915, seemingly artless best seller by Edgar Lee
Masters, must have contributed a great deal to the supposi-
tion that anyone could write in the free forms of verse.
His bare, unhighlighted style seemed almost identical
with prose and expressed the life and thought of middle

America with a directness and honesty not found in American poetry before. The book became as famous as a work of popular fiction, which in some ways it resembled. This atmosphere of feverish interest in new modes of expression explains the lengthy but insubstantial volume Amy Lowell published in 1916. *Men, Women, and Ghosts* has the merit of containing "Patterns," and it also includes some fine work in polyphonic prose: "Red Slippers," "Malmaison," and "Spring Day." Apart from these few successes, the book is largely a series of tedious experiments which test various technical possibilities of free verse, most of the poems being deficient in emotion and poetic vision.

Side by side with this frequent lack of content in her experimental poems, there is a similar defect in the story poems that now abound in Amy Lowell's books. This failing is Miss Lowell's most serious weakness since it consists in her inability to realize living characters in most of her narrative poems. Except for the last years of her life, the poet tended to be confined to her own somewhat rarefied and idiosyncratic world of thought. This was due to many causes, among them her isolation as a child, her sense of superiority, and her continual ill-health, all of which encouraged her to turn inward on herself. Some of the literary results of her introspection are of great interest, of course, but on the debit side was a habitual failure to perceive and participate in the emotional lives of others.

When we look at the narratives included in *Sword Blades and Poppy Seed*, we find it impossible to believe in any of her characters and so the poems are largely failures. In this collection, Max Breuck, the central figure in a long, carefully written poem, has no distinct qualities apart from the treatment of his starved emotions, which becomes the principal interest of this labored poem. And in the case of "The Basket" and "In A Castle," two other treatments of thwarted love, the human figures are only details in elaborate medieval settings.

The same flattening of the human elements and enlargement of the pictorial can be seen in the narrative poems of *Men, Women, and Ghosts.* In "Pickthorn Manor" and "The Cremona Violin," two studies of lost love, the emotions are sometimes well represented but the characters, as usual, are only surrogates for Miss Lowell's own inner drama. Noting the constant repetition of this motif and her statement that "neither painter nor poet chooses his subject, it is the subject that chooses him"[3] we judge that the poet's emotional balance depended on the continual reenactment of the drama of frustrated love.

Besides the failure in character portrayal, another feature of *Men, Women, and Ghosts* was significant for future developments in her work. This was her effort in Part Two of the book to picture an historical epoch through the combination of a number of independent and even disparate *tableaux.* Inadequate though it was, this was the treatment she gave to the Napoleonic era in her "Bronze Tablets," and the method was adopted for the four quasi-epics that compose her book, *Can Grande's Castle,* 1918.

Though these four poems received much praise at the time of their publication, one writer thanking God that Amy Lowell was alive, the poems are decidedly faded today, and it should be noted that the form they added to English verse has had no traceable progeny. The sources of her failure appear first of all in the polyphonic form itself of which the following passage is typical of the larger part of the book. It is taken from the second page of "Sea-Blue and Blood-Red" and follows immediately after the description of still another spectacle, that of a navy fleet at sea.

Naples
Red tiles, yellow stucco, layer on layer of windows, roofs, and balconies, Naples pushes up the hill away from the curving bay. A red, half-closed eye, Vesuvius watches and waits. All Naples prates of this and that, and runs about its little business, shouting, bawling, incessantly calling its wares . . . They even sell

water, clear crystal water for a *paul* or two. And everything done to a hullabaloo. They jabber over cheese,
they chatter over wine, they gabble at the corners in the
bright sunshine. And piercing through the noise is
the beggar-whine, always, like an undertone, the
beggar-whine; and always the crimson, watching eye
of Vesuvius.

[*CP*, 153]

The defects of the form are easily apparent. Not once do
these lines rise above the ordinary rhythms of prose, but
they are not even satisfactory in this respect, for they
are weighted with a heavy overlay of poetic devices: obtrusive internal and end-rhymes, assonance, alliteration, etc.
Miss Lowell adopted the form from the Frenchman, Paul
Fort, and maintained that she had based her version on the
"flowing cadence of oratorical prose." The failure was
partly due to her inability to recognize that prose rhythms,
however inspired, cannot substitute for the structural
firmness required in poetry. And to add a rich encrustation
of sound devices merely jars and distracts the reader. She
called her invention "polyphonic prose," a not unfitting
description. But these experiments were not useless. They
carried her investigations of free verse to their logical conclusion, and what she learned here was later applied to a
brilliant technique which is a distinctive mark of the poems
written in the last years of her life.

Fortunately, the gifts of Miss Lowell were such that she
could rise, as poet, above her theory as critic. There are a
number of effective and striking free verse passages in
these poems, but even these cannot compensate for another
defect in her conception. In *Sword Blades* and *Men, Women,
and Ghosts*, we have noted a steady flattening of the human
elements upon which story poems must depend. This process is brought to its logical extreme in *Can Grande*. In
three of the four long poems, the action is too extended
over space and time to allow for any one set of characters,

with the result that the poet focuses her attention almost entirely on physical scenes; the few figures who do appear merely illustrate the civilizations concerned. This is the clue to her unconscious intentions. These poems spring from a sense of wonder at human social achievements—and folly. Forgetting that she was a poet, not a cultural historian, she set forth to give us her sense of various epochs by means of vivid *tableaux*. The effort was a worthy one and contains a few successes, as in her description of aristocratic life at Rome (*CP*, 177-78), but read as a continuous story the poems collapse under the weight of their obtrusive detail and the lack of human emotions.

Unfortunately, the same strictures apply to her book, *Legends,* published in 1921 and a best seller in spite of these obvious weaknesses. The word "legends" is used loosely, although the poet does engage in archelogical reconstruction to give flavor to some of her scenes. Most of the poems are concerned with the theme of lost love, the best of this group being her treatment of Inca Peru in "Memorandum from a Yucca to a Passion Vine." Here Miss Lowell has used her painstaking research to create an eerie picture of the seat of the Inca Empire as well as the exotic mountain country of Peru. Another noteworthy poem is a New England ghost story, "Four Sides to a House," whose loosened ballad form is decisive evidence of the artistry which had come to the poet as the result of her constant experimentation.

During the years which saw the publication of the four books described above, Amy Lowell was also busily engaged in defending the so-called "new poetry." In its popular aspect, this took the form of readings and lecture tours which made her one of the most celebrated and controversial figures in literary America. But this was not Miss Lowell's intention. Because of her authorship of poems such as those described and her sponsorship of the three Imagist collections, questions and attacks on the new poetry were usually addressed to her. It has also been remarked that the role of public defender fell to her partly by default. Alfred Kreymborg notes in his *History of American Poetry* that there was no other literary figure qualified to play that part on this side of the ocean.[4]

In this role Amy Lowell handled herself with much success and distinction. The critical writings she produced were well designed to meet the needs of the public of her day. Though they were primarily "occasional" pieces written to fill temporary need, Miss Lowell had a real talent for discerning what was essential in the work of the new poets, and she explained their work in a manner comprehensible to the reading public as a whole. In this connection, it should be stressed that she is rightly credited with providing a rationale and focal point for the movement as a whole, most notably in her book *Tendencies in Modern American Poetry*, the bible of the early years of the movement (Damon, 426). In *Tendencies* and elsewhere she did this by recognizing the pattern of social change the poetry reflected: the breakdown of outmoded Puritan ways, in which process she championed the trend toward greater self-expression. In favoring spirit over fossilized social forms, she ranged herself on the side of the creative forces of her time, but the problem left to the future was to establish a new social equilibrium. That she foresaw the rapid changes that would follow her own lifetime is made clear in the prophetic language of "The Congressional Library" (*CP*, 452).

Such was the framework in which Miss Lowell's essays were written. As a critic she has the defects of her virtues. Like Emily Dickinson, who thought of herself as an "unlettered poet," Miss Lowell had had no education in abstract or intellectual thought. For this reason her work lacks the logic and precision required to give a fully satisfactory account of her subject matter. In dealing with questions such as free verse, her thinking reveals much unconscious confusion, and so it is impossible to know what she meant in using terms such as "cadenced verse," "metrical prose," "strophe," and "return," the last as applied to the shape of the poem as a whole.

For the same reason there is also confusion in the stand

she took on the primacy of the formal elements in poetry. In her preface to *Tendencies in Modern American Poetry,* 1917, we are told first, "Posterity cares nothing for the views that urged a man to write; to it, the poetry, its beauty as a work of art, is the only thing that matters." But then she tells us almost immediately afterwards that she will be concerned to trace "what has led each of these men to adopt the habit of mind which now characterizes him, why he has been forced out of one order into another." In the same way, in her treatment of Edwin Arlington Robinson, she first states that "Art, true art, is the desire of a man to express himself, to record the reactions of his personality to the world he lives in," but later she goes on to complain that he "never succeeds in completely omitting the writer from the thing written . . . but each volume of poems is an advance in this respect."

Side by side with these defects, there are real critical insights, especially in her long essays on Robinson and Frost. In the case of the latter, it is interesting to note that a recent volume on Frost makes frequent reference to Miss Lowell's analysis though it was written in 1916 at the very beginning of the New Englander's career.[5] *Tendencies* was the pioneer study of twentieth-century American poetry—hence of real importance in setting out the meaning and direction of advance in the new poets. Because this was her intention, it is ironical that the poet was least successful in dealing with H. D. and John Gould Fletcher, with whose work she was most in sympathy. The reason for this would appear to be the specialness of their vision. Robinson, Frost, Masters, and Sandburg (her other subjects) were primarily concerned with man in his social setting. The vision of H. D. and Fletcher was otherwise and very like her own—an impressionistic rendering of that Reality of which man's social forms are but a minor surface feature. Given Miss Lowell's incapacity for metaphysical thought, she could only fall back as critic on the treatment of the surface features of this poetry whose visionary quality she admired.

During the years in which Miss Lowell was campaigning most vigorously for the new poets, 1914-1918, she was sustained by an "intellectual energy" which Fletcher described as "unique" and was one of her most distinctive traits. For this reason, it is the more ironic that she was assailed by continual spells of illness, her long lecture tours in the East, Midwest, and South always resulting in prolonged periods of sickness and exhaustion on her return to Brookline. But this did not deter her until the summer of 1916, when she righted a small carriage after a road accident in New Hampshire. The result of this was a strain to the muscles of the abdomen which were ruptured two years later when she attempted to move a bed in a hotel room— to relieve the sleeplessness which often afflicted her. The effects of these two accidents destroyed her vitality in gradual stages over the next seven years. Between September, 1918, and May, 1921, the poet underwent four operations to repair the hernia, but without success. In the meantime severe high blood pressure developed in 1919 and this caused a worsening of the condition of her eyes when it partly subsided a few months later (Damon, 494-95). Attacks of gastric neuralgia, influenza, migraine headaches, and frequent injuries to muscles and bones caused by her bulk, continued to afflict her. Wrapped daily in an elaborate bandage to strengthen her abdomen, steadied by a cane, and aided by a basketful of eye-glasses of different strengths which she carried even on the lecture stage, the poet continued her unremitting exertions. So well did she succeed in concealing her weaknesses that no one outside her household was aware of the perilous state of her health. Having chosen a life of energetic self-assertion, she continued in this style until her vitality was entirely spent.

But this would not occur for some years to come; in the meantime, in 1919, Miss Lowell issued a new volume of impressions and lyrics which marked an important advance in her career. This book, *Pictures of the Floating World*, was composed of the forms best suited to the poet's gifts and it shows the influence of the years of study of Oriental culture which preceded its publication. A rich and striking collection, full of imagistic brilliance and invention, its only defect is its prolixity and unevenness, faults it shares with all of her books of this period. Two years after the appearance of this book, Miss Lowell also published *Fir Flower Tablets*, a collection of translations from Chinese poetry on which she had collaborated with Florence Ayscough and a Chinese scholar. Though these poems are cast too much in the form of highly colored Imagist verse, the distortion was unintentional on the part of the poet who worked with the most scupulous regard for the content and spirit of the originals. Having a deep sympathy for these poets and their civilization, she was able to recreate their work in vivid and moving language. One poem will suffice to show both the Imagist bias and the poignance with which she often invested her translations.

Together We Know Happiness
Silent and alone, I ascended the West Cupola.
The moon was like a golden hook.
In the quiet, empty, inner courtyard, the coolness of
    early autumn enveloped the wu-tung tree.

Scissors cannot cut this thing;
Unravelled, it joins again and clings.
It is the sorrow of separation,
And none other tastes to the heart like this.

[*CP*, 357]

Most of what has been said above about the poems of Amy Lowell between the years 1913 and 1921 has been of a negative character. It is, in short, the case that could reasonably be lodged against her, however various and inconsistent the actual criticisms have been. It is also a one-sided presentation, as I have already shown. A poet who could write "The Camellia Tree of Matsue" as spontaneously as a wide-eyed child, is entitled to be judged by her merits, not by the instances where her talents were misapplied. In the remainder of this chapter and in the one that follows, the emphasis will be on individual poems from her Imagist period, and the purpose will be to suggest the types of literary excellence they represent.

II

Alpine Spring and Temple Bells

For those reading *Sword Blades and Poppy Seed* in 1914 and coming upon "The Captured Goddess," the most striking feature of the poem would have been its highly irregular form. There was no rhyme-scheme and almost no rhyme. Some lines consisted of but one or two words and the length of the stanzas varied from one line to twelve. Compared to the tidy quatrains of the Victorians or their sonnets and blank verse, such a poem gives an impression of lawlessness and the use of this form aroused great hostility in Amy Lowell's time among the defenders of the safe, old ways.

Such is the power of convention. It might be more sensible to reverse the proposition and ask for a justification of such arbitrary devices as the ornate French forms, rime royal, or even the iambic pentameter which Shakespeare himself all but abandoned at the height of his powers. Anything which is severely styled must, by its very nature, lose many expressive possibilities. This is a serious objection which may be lodged against traditional verse forms. As W. P. Ker has pointed out, the function of these forms is more than merely passive—as containers of poetic ideas. Like the orchestra which controls the movements of dancers, they set up tunes to which the thought of the poet must dance.[6]

All this would be merely academic if there were no alternative means to organize a poem. But this is not the case as shown by the large body of good poetry written in the last six decades in a form called free verse. Many persons have tried to develop a formula for poetry of this kind without arriving at satisfactory results. The explanation appears to lie in the nature of artistic creation. A poem which is more than a versified thought is the product of an esthetic impulse, a controlling pattern or *gestalt*. This impulse determines the rhythms of a poem and so lifts even metrical verse from a mechanical regularity. In free verse, no arbitrary, preexistent pattern is involved, so the design of the poem is simply the fulfillment of this impulse. As Emerson once wrote, it is not meter that makes a poem, "but a meter-making argument."

For these reasons no generalized scheme can be applied to free verse, either in the writing of it or its analysis. As students, the best that we can do is to note the particular devices that a writer has used to give structure, beauty, and coherence to his poem. The comments of Roger Fry on the art of Paul Klee apply equally well to the organicism of free verse:

> It is almost certain that in these intimate rhythms that make up the texture of a work of art, in those parts which are due to the artist's sensibility, we pass into regions which elude all mathematical statement, as indeed do all but the simplest organic forms. We pass from rigid and exact relations to complex and endlessly varying rhythms, which we may perhaps be allowed to call, hypothetically, vital rhythms, through which the artist's subconscious feelings reveal themselves to us by what we call his sensibility.[7]

The seeming oddity involved in the notion of *free* verse disappears if we grasp the inseparability of language and esthetic patterning. Everyone who speaks English gives his words a rhythmic design in the instant of their utterance. They would be inchoate sounds otherwise, and all written prose is similarly stylized up to and including the complex effects of poetic prose. The design is produced intuitively, according to the speaker's "ear," without the benefit of the clearly marked forms and limits which exist in metrical poetry. Given the verbal gifts of the poet, it is not surprising that some of them are able to apply the same intuitive faculty to the creation of novel and satisfying patterns of verse.

The structure of such poetry is organic, that is, it follows the shape of the poet's thought with the result that no two poems will have the same form. Less musical in the sense of regular chiming, its advantage over meter consists in its economy and range of expression. After seven decades of organic art forms in the dance, architecture, painting, etc., it seems clear that Hulme was right in believing, as he did, that mental images exist for which fixed forms are a bed of Procrustes.[8] "The Captured Goddess," the poem which elicited this discussion, would appear to be such an image. It is difficult to imagine this ethereal poem taking shape for us in anything other than these weightless and transparent lines of free verse:

> Over the housetops,
> Above the rotating chimney-pots,
> I have seen a shiver of amethyst,
> And blue and cinnamon have flickered
> A moment,
> At the far end of a dusty street.
>
> Through sheeted rain
> Has come a lustre of crimson,
> And I have watched moonbeams
> Hushed by a film of palest green.
> It was her wings,
> Goddess!
> Who stepped over the clouds,
> And laid her rainbow feathers
> Aslant on the currents of the air.

In this opening passage, we should note the unusual delicacy of the sound patterning. Free verse is free only of the restraints of fixed forms. Miss Lowell used her freedom to create rhythms that give a sense of airy, unfettered movement; what she is envisioning is preternatural and it is afloat in the air.

Apart from the upturned rhythms, especially in the first two lines, the language which supports this vision is composed of subtle interweavings of sound: the o's in the two opening lines, the slant rhyme in top and pot, the measured recurrence of s's and t's which draws together the passage as a whole; and the division into short lines which contributes to the sense of airiness and evanescence.

Having created this vision of a divine beauty which transfigures the world, the poet proceeds to deepen her effect by describing the emotions which it produced—and the manifestation of the divinity in varied physical forms.

> I followed her for long,
> With gazing eyes and stumbling feet.
> I cared not where she led me,
> My eyes were full of colors:
> Saffrons, rubies, the yellows of beryls,
> And the indigo-blue of quartz;
> Flights of rose, layers of chrysoprose,
> Points of orange, spirals of vermilion,
> The spotted gold of tiger-lily petals,
> The loud pink of bursting hydrangeas,
> I followed,
> And watched for the flashing of her wings.

In the opening lines of the poem the vision of the reader was directed upward to patterns of light in the sky. In this passage we are concerned with the experience and actions of the poet on earth, her rapid forward movement being conveyed in end-stopped lines with strong final stresses. She is drawn forward tirelessly by her hypnotic absorption in a Presence glimpsed innumerable times on earth in the allure of color, flower forms, and even in precious stones. Her list is followed by an abrupt return to the goddess herself, the source and meaning of all this beauty. In the last section of the poem, the poet treats one of the central paradoxes of life. Though divine in nature like the goddess, a thing may still be left unprotected in the divine scheme of things, subject to shipwreck:

> In the city I found her,
> The narrow-streeted city.
> In the market-place I came upon her,
> Bound and trembling.
> Her fluted wings were fastened to her sides
>   with cords,
> She was naked and cold,
> For that day the wind blew
> Without sunshine.
>
> Men chaffered for her,
> They bargained in silver and gold,
> In copper, in wheat,
> And called their bids across the market-place.
>
> The Goddess wept.
>
> Hiding my face I fled,
> And the grey wind hissed behind me,
> Along the narrow streets.

[*CP*, 31-32]

The subtle art controlling the form and movement of this poem may be seen here in the placement of e, s, er, and i sounds, whose interweaving produces a very musical effect. The rhythms are as hurried as ever in their tracing of the poet's breathless pursuit, but the scene that closes the poem introduces a harsh, discordant note and this is expressed in the sharply cut edges of these lines. There is a sensible withdrawal of feeling as the poet recoils before the vision

of the Goddess bound over to the hands of men and offered
as an item of sale in the marketplace.

In this celebration of a divine beauty accompanied by
the emotions of religious worship, the poem recalls "Before The Altar" and can be seen as a variant of a major
theme that Miss Lowell treats in "The Slippers of the
Goddess of Beauty" discussed above and in "Fool O' The
Moon," another poem from the end of her career (*CP*, 465).
"The Captured Goddess" appears to be the best of this
group. It presents the mystical experience itself instead of
the general statements about it we find in the poems before her Imagist phase. It has this same advantage over
"The Slippers," although this is effective as a long-medi-
tated and deeply felt restatement of her attitude written at
the end of her life. As for "Fool O' The Moon," the feeling
here is also intense and immediate, but the emotions of
religious adoration are mixed with those of sexual desire.
This is clearly not the case in "The Captured Goddess."
The emotion and its expression are self-contained and austere, the effect of a deep-seated attitude of mind revealed
in these poems of her early Imagist phase. Nowhere is it
expressed to better effect than in her sonnet, "Irony," a
composition in wavering monochrome.

An arid daylight shines along the beach
Dried to a grey monotony of tone,
And stranded jelly-fish melt soft upon
The sun-baked pebbles, far beyond their reach
Sparkles a wet, reviving sea. Here bleach
The skeletons of fishes, every bone
Polished and stark, like traceries of stone,
The joints and knuckles hardened each to each.
And they are dead while waiting for the sea,
The moon-pursuing sea, to come again.
Their hearts are blown away on the hot breeze.
Only the shells and stones can wait to be
Washed bright. For living things, who suffer pain,
May not endure till time can bring them ease.
                                                        [*CP*, 37]

This poem has almost the air of clinical analysis and part of its effect consists in the refusal to flinch before so desolating a vision. What she offers in "Irony" is the Zen garden of gravel, sand, and rock, and like those gardens in Japan, it is a vision of the eternal frame of things. If such a scheme makes no allowance for the finite living thing and refreshes stones and shells only, it still contains an undeniable magnificence. The mid-day sun not only scorches the jelly-fish, it also fills the beach with light, and there is an implication of grandeur in the unusual formal harmony of this poem. Aside from the consistency in tone and image, the harmony is due to the rhythms which transcend the rigid iambic pattern to form a single unbroken curve. It is also due to the consistency in language and, within that, an unobtrusive skein of s, b, and p sounds which draws together the poem as a whole. Taste in poetry differs with each reader, but with a poem such as this, one must concede at least the perfection of the style. In "Irony" the mood of the poet and the severity of the sonnet form she chose have combined to produce a poem of remarkable expressive force.

The same quality of expression applied to a related theme can be found in the poem, "Convalescence," which also appeared in *Sword Blades and Poppy Seed*. In this poem the victim who suffers is as solitary and abandoned as the sea creatures in "Irony," but here we have the adequate response. The swimmer who toils toward the "rounding beach" is the equal, in Miss Lowell's vision, of the ocean, an idea implied by the juxtaposition of his perfect silhouette against the ocean waters. Moreover, he succeeds in his struggle, and her account of this and the various luminosities of the seashore is one of the most vivid passages in her poetry.

> So up, and down, and forward, inch by inch,
> He gains upon the shore, where poppies glow
> And sandflies dance their little lives away.
> The sucking waves retard, and tighter clinch

The weeds about him, but the land-winds blow,
And in the sky there blooms the sun of May.

The "but" in the penultimate line of this poem is a
significant one. The individual may be erased by hostile
forces, but it is evident that this does not limit or define the
possibilities of life. In "A Tulip Garden," at least, it is
triumphant, an inexplicable splendor whose crashing
chords are yet unheard by us.

> . . . Our ears are dead,
> We cannot catch the tune. In pantomime
> Parades that army. With our utmost powers
> We hear the wind stream through a bed of flowers.
>
> [*CP*, 74]

The life that thawed in "Convalescence" and warmed
briefly in "A Tulip Garden" is as exposed as ever in "The
Temple," but here it has discovered its inner nature and has
achieved an equilibrium with the forces that would assail
it. This sonnet, admirable for the force and expressiveness
of its rhythms, is a dramatic image of the mysterious birth
of an attachment which transforms two lives. Its subject is
the friendship between Mrs. Russell and Amy Lowell, but
the poem is far from being either intimate in feeling or
sentimental. It is, rather, the revelation of an elemental
force no less tremendous because we have diluted it into
many unmeaning forms.

> Between us leapt a gold and scarlet flame.
> Into the hollow of the cupped, arched blue
> Of heaven it rose. Its flickering tongues updrew
> And vanished in the sunshine. How it came
> We guessed not, nor what thing could be its name.
> From each to each had sprung these sparks which flew
> Together into fire. . . .

These lines leave no doubt as to the spirituality of a love
which sweeps irresistibly upward. But the paradox im-

plied in "The Captured Goddess" continues in force. The flame which rose instantly to its source in heaven must be closely guarded from the scheme of things on earth, and in the remaining half of the poem we have the image of the building of a temple-fortress where man's art and determination are able to hold off the forces inimical to a divine attachment.

Miss Lowell's relationship with Ada Russell is also the subject of two admirable free verse lyrics, "Anticipation" and "The Taxi," which appear in this same volume. All three of these poems illustrate Amy Lowell's characteristic mode as dramatic lyricist. Though her lyrical impulse was strong, her short poems of personal feeling do not ordinarily sing. There were few occasions in her life for simple feeling, nor would a pure lyric utterance do justice to her exploratory vision. For these reasons she drew on her sense of the dramatic to produce a hybrid form. By this I mean that her personal emotions are usually objectified to some extent by translation into picture and narrative elements. While this sometimes led to diffuseness, a besetting sin in Amy Lowell, in other instances it gives unusual force and concreteness to the expression of intangible inner states. An example of this, both in its sharply focused images and the use of story to develop emotion, can be found in "The Taxi." Here, as in "The Captured Goddess," the free verse of Miss Lowell is so purely conceived and lithe that it has a plastic, statuesque character:

> When I go away from you
> The world beats dead
> Like a slackened drum.
> I call out for you against the jutted stars
> And shout into the ridges of the wind.
> Streets coming fast,
> One after the other,
> Wedge you away from me,
> And the lamps of the city prick my eyes

So that I can no longer see your face.
Why should I leave you,
To wound myself upon the sharp edges of
    the night?

[*CP*, 43]

Even more affecting, perhaps, but less even in quality
of writing, is her poem, "Patience," which was written
about Ada a short time after their relationship had been
established on a permanent basis. Here, more directly than
in the other poems of this collection, Miss Lowell has
given the sense of an awakening to spring in some Alpine
fastness—

Be patient with you?
When the snow-girt earth
Cracks to let through a spurt
Of sudden green, and from the muddy dirt
A snowdrop leaps, how mark its worth
To eyes frost-hardened, and do weary men
Feel patience then?

In 1914 Miss Lowell's emotional life had been numbed
and chilled. At its best, as in poems such as "The Captured Goddess" and "Irony," it was also of a glassy purity.
By the time that *Pictures of the Floating World* was published in 1919, Mrs. Russell had served with Amy for five
years, her first close human tie in a life of more than forty
years. In this same period of time Miss Lowell had also
won belated success as a poet. As the result the character
of her emotions changed. The poet had become more fully
herself. Her feelings and so the forms which expressed them
in her poetry became more extended, often swelling in
outline, at times even serene.

There is also the difference in outlook occasioned by her
Oriental studies. These had begun in earnest in 1917 when
she and Florence Ayscough had decided to collaborate in
the translation of Chinese poetry. The wide-ranging re-

search that followed deepened her response to a civilization in which art had ordered and refined the whole conduct of life. This was the concept of the Orient developed by Percival Lowell, her brother, and Amy's identification with Oriental life follows the lines of this thought.

Through her choice of an epigraph for *Sword Blades and Poppy Seed* Miss Lowell confides that she has been concerned to produce images of the Divinity, the "invisible face," which looks out of all nature. In the poems described above the individual is set against a Supernatural primarily hostile to man's desires, though it clothes itself in awesome beauty. In the poems of the Oriental phase, the power of art appears to mediate between the solitary individual and the Absolute. This is still essentially hostile to man, but now his life is dignified with ritual that ennobles it and sets him in the scheme of the Divine. This is what we see in "Reflections," a poem equally divided between attention to a transcendent beauty which invests the garden landscape and tragic unfulfillment expressed in the figure seated by the lake. Here the poet is both observed and observer, the lady into whose eyes she looks being herself:

> When I looked into your eyes,
> I saw a garden
> With peonies, and tinkling pagodas,
> And round-arched bridges
> Over still lakes.
> A woman sat beside the water
> In a rain-blue silken garment.
> She reached through the water
> To pluck the crimson peonies
> Beneath the surface,
> But as she grasped the stems,
> They jarred and broke into white-green ripples;
> And as she drew out her hand,
> The water-drops dripping from it
> Stained her rain-blue dress like tears.
>
> [*CP*, 208]

Though Miss Lowell was often a romantic, this poem is evidence that she could summon the restraint necessary to the control of tragic emotions. Nothing could be more reticent than these lines. The broken life is expressed only through the jarring of the water lilies, and the drops which stain the dress of the victim come from the lake, not her eyes. Much of the effectiveness of "Reflections" depends on a sparseness of detail allowing the reader to build the symbolic images which are the real content of Miss Lowell's poetry. Taken simply as description, such pictures would signally fail. Close attention shows an incompleteness in this respect, exemplified here by the presentation of this elaborate garden-scene in four short lines. In place of an approximation of reality the effect that Miss Lowell achieves with her economy of language, the use of suspended rhythms that have the static quality of the lake and her few, well chosen details is the evocation of the spirit of the scene, the Numinous in the forms of the flowers, in the sound of the temple bells, and the unmelting figure at the side of the lake. Clothed in this way in these congenial Oriental forms, it is a more resonant image and a more delicate one than anything in the earlier poems. The crimson peonies glow brightly against the rain-blue dress, and the architecture of the verse has relaxed from the angularity found in "Irony."

The rise to organic form and the fullest extension of emotion are to be found in "Free Fantasia on Japanese Themes," a brilliant treatment of the theme of deprivation. Here, the self is no longer shattered as in some of the poems collected in *A Dome*. It is triumphant in self-assertion, but the powerful energies released have no emotional outlet except in fantasy. The fulfillment of the poet's desires is entirely imaginary, and it is represented in a picturesque, Oriental setting.

> I would experience new emotions—
> Submit to strange enchantments—
> Bend to influences,

Bizarre, exotic,
Fresh with burgeoning.

I would climb a sacred mountain,
Struggle with other pilgrims up a steep path through
    pine-trees,
Above to the smooth, treeless slopes,
And prostrate myself before a painted shrine,
Beating my hands upon the hot earth,
Quieting my eyes upon the distant sparkle
Of the faint spring sea. . . .

This is the poet who had written in one of her first poems,

I weary for desires never guessed,
For alien passions, strange imaginings,
To be some other person for a day.

[*CP*, 20]

And "Free Fantasia" can be seen as an Imagist version of
that same theme. What is asked is not freedom for self-
indulgence but to advance to the center of life. This desire
accounts for the attraction Miss Lowell felt for the intense
artistic life of the East. But at the end of the poem after
other such imaginings as she gives us above, she returns
to her home, and her verses follow this movement in their
shift to a static and hollow tone:

I would anything
Rather than this cold paper;
With outside, the quiet sun on the sides of burgeoning
    branches,
And inside, only my books.

[*CP*, 219]

The powerful rhythms generated by the emotions of this
poem contrast with the suavity of expression found in
"Solitaire," a free verse poem of closely related theme. Here,

suppleness of rhythm and sound-patterning as in the placement of s, b, p, and l sounds, the graceful movement of its thought, and the radiance of its dream landscape combine to suggest the effect of a Debussy nocturne. As regular and perfectly articulated as a sonnet, the poem is proof of the highly wrought formal beauty to which free verse may rise in her hands.

> When night drifts along the streets of the city,
> And sifts down between the uneven roofs,
> My mind begins to peek and peer.
> It plays at ball in old, blue Chinese gardens,
> And shakes wrought dice-cups in Pagan temples
> Amid the broken flutings of white pillars.
> It dances with purple and yellow crocuses in its hair,
> And its feet shine as they flutter over drenched grasses.
> How light and laughing my mind is,
> When all good folk have put out their bedroom candles,
> And the city is still!
>
> [*CP*, 218]

The meaning of "Solitaire" is contained in its implied statements on human imagination. Miss Lowell suggests that this offers not only a substitute for real-life events but experiences possible only to the spirit itself, hence the delicate texture of the poem. Like the lines of "The Captured Goddess" intended to evoke Divinity, this is a tissue of words which floats free of ordinary physical moorings. The poem resembles "Free Fantasia" in that both are treatments of Miss Lowell's life of fantasy, and they show the refinement of sensation gained by her study of the Orient. Free of the weight of the body and the limits of place, the mind rejoices in its ability to encompass essences for which the images in these poems are emblems.

Very like "Solitaire" in its brevity and precision, the surrealist "Haunted" is a dream-vision of another kind (*CP*, 216). A terrifying account of sexual violation, it is Amy Lowell's involuntary witness to what is sinister and

predacious in nature. That the poet intended to generalize
her narrative in this way is shown in the imagery which
concludes the poem with its links to all experience of
covert evil and terror:

> Hark! A hare is strangling in the forest,
> And the wind tears a shutter from the wall.

The sexual imagery of "Haunted" prepares us to some
extent for one of the most exuberant and effective of Miss
Lowell's visions. In its cumbrous title, "Little Ivory
Figures Pulled With A String," Miss Lowell impugns
the intellectual who would deny the Dionysian sources
of human vitality, which she prefigures in the imagery of
the opening stanza. Having set her scene in a Mediterranean garden cafe where the stiff "puppet" is seated, she
makes a rapid shift to a hallucinatory vision:

> String your blood to chord with this music,
> Stir your heels upon the cobbles to the rhythm of a
>   dance-tune,
> They have slim thighs and arms of silver;
> The moon washes away their garments;
> They make a pattern of fleeing feet in the branch
>   shadows,
> And the green grapes knotted about them
> Burst as they press against one another. . . .

The strategy of the poem is to move alternately between
the image of this dionysian revel and that of the constrained
intellectual. In the concluding part, there is a direct re-
proof to one who "would drink" only from his brains, and
finally the fusion of the two motifs in a passage of climactic
intensity:

> Rise up on the music,
> Fling against the moon-drifts in a whorl of young
>   light bodies:

Leaping grape-clusters,
Vine leaves tearing from a grey wall.
You shall run, laughing, in a braid of women,
And weave flowers with the frosty spines of thorns.
Why do you gaze into your glass,
And jar the spoons with your finger-tapping?
The rain is rigid on the plates of my heart.
The murmur of it is loud—loud.   [*CP*, 236]

"Penumbra," another lyric from this period, is the very
reverse of this orgiastic vision. One of the most tenuous
of Miss Lowell's poems, it is an extended meditation which
builds beautiful effects from a verse pattern that all but
duplicates an unadorned, conversational speech. It is marked
off from prose by the nice balance of phrasing in long
cadences which seem to move to a rarefied music of the
inner ear. The subject of the poem is the attachment between
Ada Russell and Miss Lowell, a poignant emotion on both
sides. In this poem the emotional bond not only unites the
two women but it insinuates itself through their physical
setting, drawing everything together into the single harmony which is the essence of the poem.

The old house will guard you,
As I have done.
Its walls and rooms will hold you,
And I shall whisper my thoughts and fancies
As always,
From the pages of my books.
You will sit here, some quiet summer night,
Listening to the puffing trains,
But you will not be lonely,
For these things are a part of me.
And my love will go on speaking to you
Through the chairs, and the tables, and the
      pictures,
As it does now through my voice,
And the quick, necessary touch of my hand.
                                            [*CP*, 217]

An emotion such as this is fragile, as are the circumstances upon which it depends. Acknowledging this in the very cadences of her verse, she has yet had the art to recreate its wistful, diaphanous beauty.

The account of the poems of Miss Lowell's middle phase could be extended indefinitely. *Pictures of the Floating World* contains a variety of vividly conceived subjects, but their power usually resides in suggestion rather than paraphraseable statement. So we may conclude with a comment made by the poet herself to explain her highly elusive "Violin Sonata by Vincent D' Indy" inscribed to her musician friend, Charles Martin Loeffler (*CP*, 220). For many readers the poem would only be a description of Loeffler playing the violin in his home, though the atmosphere is eerie and there is a reference to the sawing of flesh "against the cold blue gates of the sky." In discussing her poem in the Boston *Transcript*, Miss Lowell remarked, "I meant to give the limits of humanity seeking to spiritualize itself to accord with its conception of Deity, which is D' Indy's very idiom, it seems to me" (Damon, 507). This comment along with the epigraphs she chose for her first two books of poems show that Miss Lowell was aware of the pattern of symbolic meanings sketched in this chapter. After giving her novel interpretation of the music of D' Indy, which she sees as expressive of man's upward reach toward God, she adds the telling phrase, "it seems to me." The fact that art and man showed themselves in these terms to her imagination *would seem to be* her best claim to survival as a poet.

Chapter Five

John Keats and High Noon

Last Poems: 1922-1925

I

Nemesis

When Amy Lowell's friend, John Gould Fletcher, visited the United States in 1922, he found the poet at a library in New York energetically at work on research for her Keats's biography. In his eyes she seemed as vivid and charming as ever. Miss Lowell's outward appearance had changed little since they met in 1913, and she was still the "tireless scholar" in search of new knowledge. Having emerged from the literary battles of 1914-1918 as the most influential American poet, she had become a best seller in 1919 with the publication of her fifth book of verse, and by 1922 was regarded as a "national institution" whose slow and labored approach to a speaker's lectern was the signal for the audience to rise.

By 1922, movement of any kind was hazardous and difficult for Miss Lowell. The failure of her first operation for hernia in 1918 led to a new attempt, more trying for the patient, whose good effects were undone almost at once by a mishap that befell her in March, 1920 (Damon, 528). The massive third operation, in October, performed by a team of five surgeons, was first believed to be a success, until new alarms in early 1921. In the meantime in August, 1920, still in relatively normal health, Miss Lowell had looked about her and described the luckless state to which she had been brought. The quotation is from a letter to her brother, the president of Harvard, then in England to receive honorary degrees from Oxford and Cambridge:

> My hernia is getting rather painful again. I am to see the New York doctor in September. I know very well that they will advise another operation, and none of them guarantees a success, and I myself believe that one might have any number of these operations, but I do not think there is any real hope of cure in my case.

They all tell me that this is a very difficult thing to
cure, and my age and size are against me, but to feel
perfectly well and energetic and be tied by a little
local thing of that sort is hard. Dr. Porter even says
that I ought not to go on a sea voyage without an
operation for fear of strangulation, which, of course,
although not extremely likely . . . is quite possible.
I do think that I have had enough illness in my life,
and it is hard to keep up a career and do all you want
to do under these difficulties. Of course we manage
somehow, meanwhile I try not to think about it any-
more than I can help. . . .

[Damon, 554-55]

The surgery in October, 1920, and a fourth operation which
followed in May, 1921, only weakened her further so that
the poet's life was seriously endangered. Her survival
would depend on her ability to restrict her activity—and
at the same time to find labors capable of distracting her
mind from facts which had long been intolerable to it.

This should not have been impossible. Already at hand
were a multitude of interests and projects, sufficient to
occupy her for some years. But in the first month of 1921,
the two purposes came into direct collision. At that time
Professor William Lyon Phelps asked Miss Lowell to
deliver the Keats centenary address at Yale. Since the poet
had been a devotee of Keats from the age of fifteen and had
put together one of the largest collections of his manuscripts in existence, it was natural that she would accept
the opportunity to use her special knowledge and sources
of information.

The lecture was a success, and when she was asked to
publish it, Miss Lowell decided instead to expand her essay
in the form of a book-length psychological study. The
project seemed harmless and unexacting. She would draw
on the unpublished letters and other matter available in
the United States and use her own insights to enlarge the
understanding of his life. Besides, it was a fact that her

other prose works had been very speedily and easily written. They were not slight, but they were forensical in nature, the product of her keen wits and life-long training in Lowell family debate.

Her fourth operation for hernia delayed this project and during her convalescence in June and July, 1921, she proved once more that she could write quickly and well. At the suggestion of her brother, Lawrence, she wrote a sequel to *A Fable For Critics*, 1848, by James Russell Lowell. Composed in a humorous and light-hearted vein, her book is notable for the giddiness of its rhymes ("stopped dead" and "pop from his head"), and the deliberate mockery contained in the jiggling movement of its long-winded lines. In spite of this comical manner, or partly because of it, the book succeeds as a unique addition to the literature of the period. Turning its pages, the reader obtains a more vivid impression of the writers of the "poetic remaissance," as it was called, than he is likely to find in any other account. *A Critical Fable* is all that remains today of the spirited talk in Miss Lowell's library at Sevenels, her language continually uplifted on fanciful bursts of simile and metaphor. A good example is her exuberant account of John Gould Fletcher which leaves no doubt about her taste for highly colored impressionism (*CP*, 416-18). In her six-page account of herself, she adopts the point of view of the many critics who found her fantastic and extravagant:

> Armed to the teeth like an old Samurai,
> Juggling with jewels like the ancient genii,
> Hung all over with mouse-traps of metres, and cages
> Of bright-plumaged rhythms, with pages and pages
> Of colours slit up into streaming confetti
> Which give the appearance of something sunsetty
> And gorgeous, and flowing—a curious sight
> She makes in her progress, a modern White Knight,
> Forever explaining her latest inventions
> And assuring herself of all wandering attentions

By pausing at times to sing, in a duly
Appreciative manner, an aria from Lully . . .

[*CP*, 411]

This book contains portraits of all the notables of the day,
that is, twenty-one poets in Miss Lowell's estimation. A
feast of keen wit and insight, the poet was clearly wrong
only in her judgment of the lyrics of Edna St. Vincent
Millay.

After completing *A Critical Fable* during her two month
convalescence, the poet turned with gusto to her research
on Keats. Her plan was to complete the book by the spring
of 1922. But the writing phase did not even begin until
the fall of that year and even then she found that the process had to be interrupted anew by periods of further research. Some of these scholarly duties were of the most
formidable kind, and already in November, 1922, she had
formed the habit of working as much as eighteen hours a
day to hasten her labors. By the end of December of that
year, Damon states that the poet was near exhaustion.

The explanation for this can be found in the new character which her study took almost from the beginning of
her research. From the presentation of a modernist point
of view on Keats and especially on the maligned Fanny
Brawne, Amy Lowell's work expanded to a total biographical reconstruction. No fact regarding his poetry or
his life was too small to be pursued and then stuck tri-
umphantly on the canvas. An idea of what this involved
may be gained from the history she gives for the Keats's
poem "In Drear-Nighted December." She tells us that Keats
had stayed at Burford Bridge after he completed *Endymion*,
and that on one of his last days there, he wrote this "little
lyric":

This poem has had rather a curious history, which
it seems worth-while to retail in full. In the first place,
in Woodhouse's testimony, it was attributed to the
year 1818; but the discovery of the second Woodhouse

Commonplace Book (*Poems* II), corrected what was all along an error on Woodhouse's part, for in that volume he carefully revises his former judgment by recording that Jane Reynolds had told him that it was written in December, 1817, while Keats was at Burford Bridge. The poem was published in the *Gem*, a periodical edited by Thomas Hood, in 1829, and, in the same year, made one of the selections from Keats's work in the Galignani edition of the *Poems of Coleridge, Shelley, and Keats.* These practically contemporaneous printings have hitherto been supposed to be the first. I am, however, indebted to a correspondent in the London *Times Literary Supplement,* for a still further correction. It seems that some two or three weeks before its appearance in the *Gem*, the poem, in a slightly different version, was printed in the *Literary Gazette* for September nineteenth, 1829. There it was put in the selection *Original Poetry*, entitled merely *Stanzas (Unpublished)* and signed at the end "John Keats." Later, in the number for October twenty-fourth, 1829, at the end of a review of the *Gem*, the gazette reviewer remarked: "There is a poem of the late J. Keats, which appeared a few weeks since in the *Literary Gazette:* it is but justice to state that the proprietors had previously printed their version from another copy."[1]

Fortunately, this sort of microscopic detail is not typical of the book as a whole, and it is quoted only to show the thoroughness of Miss Lowell's scholarship. The same thoroughness applied to Keats's life as a whole made it possible for her to establish a firm chronology for the writing of his poems and almost as much for his day-to-day existence. These were real achievements and the findings concerned are the basis of present-day scholarship on the poet. But one may still doubt whether the results justified her exertions. Almost from the beginning of her writing there was a decline in her health, evident in loss of weight, reduced energy, and impaired eyesight (Damon, 626). And as she pored endlessly over minute details in

Keats's draft manuscripts, the crabbed writing of his marginal notes, and the many unpublished letters she had found, she was left with little time or energy for her own poetry.

In view of all this one may ask why the poet did not call a temporary halt at the end of 1923 when she finally completed the first half of her massive 1,200 page work. The most likely explanation is that she was aware of the danger to her health and sought to avoid collapse by hurrying the work to a conclusion. In any event, she could not give up. If she feared that her hour was about to strike— hence the title which she gave to *What's O' Clock*—that was all the more reason to wish to complete her tribute to the beloved poet. The result of this was a book uniquely satisfying as a reconstruction of literary and biographical fact but offering only the minimum of interpretation and art in the disposition of its unwieldy materials. Such as it was, however, it earned the following tribute in a letter from John Middleton Murry to Florence Ayscough regarding a memorial service for Miss Lowell in England:

                                                    Dorset
                                              April 5, 1926
Dear Mrs. Ayscough:

   I am very sorry indeed that I cannot be present at your meeting. Had I been in London I should have counted it my bounden duty to add my tribute to the magnificent work upon Keats done by your dear friend, Miss Amy Lowell—a duty the more obligatory because I feel that it has received but a grudging acknowledgment from English criticism. . . . No one who has not made a patient study of Keats' life and work can possibly know what Miss Lowell has done in her magnum opus. . . . I, who hold a very different view of Keats' from Miss Lowell's, should like to put on record my conviction that she has written the final biography of Keats. Subsequent generations will, I think, alter and amend her critical views;

but the substance of all future attempts to recreate Keats in his habit as he lived will be the work of Miss Amy Lowell. . . .[2]

If the book on Keats was overly diffuse, the reverse was true for her best poetry of this period. In these same years Miss Lowell had entered her most distinguished phase as poet, largely discarding her Orientalism in favor of an idiom which was more dense and spontaneous. Where formerly plastic values had been dominant, as she sought to reveal the inner shape of things, now we find a greater abstractness and angularity, shown in her extensive use of meter, as she turns to reflection and introspective states. Like the shift from the style of *Sword Blades* to that of *Pictures*, the tendency to a more concentrated style is evidence that the form of her art was dictated by changes in her thought as she moved through the various stages of her career.

However that may be, beginning in 1920 Amy Lowell began to produce a sizeable number of striking poems which must be considered her best work. The research she undertook on Keats carried her by association back to another favored "landscape," that of medieval England, and the intensity of her response to this, like her sympathy for the Orient, is responsible for the color and tapestry-like effect of many of these poems. In this respect there is a resemblance between Miss Lowell and Henry James. Though she would never have disdained her country as he sometimes did, she resembled James in that she could not embody her visions in an unfurnished landscape. In the poetry preceding her study of the Orient, there had also been a large element of medievalism in her work. In one poem of this period she reveals the charm she had found in "faded, old world" things.

They soothe us like a song, heard in a garden sung
By youthful minstrels, on the moonlight flung

In cadences and falls, to ease a queen,
Widowed and childless, cowering in a screen
Of myrtles, whose life hangs with all its strings
    unstrung.   [*CP*, 33]

This was a positive effect of her work on Keats. A more
crucial one was the fact that it reduced the time she had
available to write poems. There was a two week "poetry-
burst," as she called it, in July, 1923, and at the very end
of that year, ill in bed, she composed a group of poems inspired by Eleonora Duse. But there was no time for sustained
efforts after that. This meant not only that fewer poems
were written but some of her best have come to us with untidy blemishes. "Alice Meynell," for instance, has verses
which are only in rough draft and the same is true of a few
lines in "Evelyn Ray." These two are among her best and
most serious efforts, and so it is reasonable to suppose that
the flaws were the result of her haste.

The need to make the most of her work-days was due,
of course to her desire to finish the writing of *John Keats*,
but this massive labor had now taken charge of her life.
Before she had completed the task in December, 1924, the
work had consumed more than three years of her life, and
her last photograph taken at about this time shows the
fatal effects on her health.[3] At some point in those endless
labors the poet had lost her vitality, but even in the winter
of 1924 when her condition began to alarm Mrs. Russell
and other intimates, Miss Lowell looked forward hopefully
to a gradual recovery of her strength. *Keats* was published
in February, 1925, and became a best seller at once. In
April Miss Lowell was to begin a three-month lecture
tour of England where she would defend her biography
and her modernist poetry before her critics in that country.

Accordingly, a farewell banquet was held for her on
April 4, attended by leading citizens of Boston. Six days
later, on Good Friday, she was dictating letters to her sec-
retaries when she was seized by "a terrible pain." The
abdominal muscles had begun to separate, but her doctors
thought it unwise to operate. Afflicted by nausea in the

weeks that followed she slowly starved to death, but even in this extremity she continued to write letters and to sit in her library for a few minutes each day. On May 12, the day before the long postponed operation, she was seated before her mirror when she saw the right side of her face drop and knew her own death. An hour and a half later, attended by a doctor and Mrs. Russell, she succumbed to a stroke. The warm season being already advanced, lilacs were in bloom in Miss Lowell's park and large clumps of these were placed about her body in the library. Three days later her ashes were interred in Mount Auburn, and a great futility, which had pervaded American poetry for two decades before 1912, began to settle again.

II

Harvest

Whatever ended that day at Mount Auburn, it was not the life of Amy Lowell's poetry. In the years which immediately followed her death, three new volumes were issued, *What's O'Clock*, 1925, *East Wind*, 1926, and *Ballads For Sale*, 1927, all taken from her bulging folders of unpublished material. Though they varied a great deal in quality, each gave evidence of the new powers of expression which the poet had acquired in the last few years of her life.

The poems of *East Wind* were the first in order of time, the poet having worked on this manuscript as early as 1921. A collection of tales of rural New England life, the thirteen poems continue the vein of gloom begun in "The Overgrown Pasture" sequence of *Men, Women, and Ghosts.* The peculiarity of these compositions is the lack of poetic quality in their form. In her zeal for innovation, Amy Lowell had devised a flat, free verse monologue whose jaggedness and use of dialect she hoped to turn to expressive account. The form justifies itself to a certain extent in "Off The Turnpike" and "Number Three On The Docket" from the earlier book. Both of these poems are studies of mental derangement produced by loneliness and emotional repression. As characters, Hiram's widow in the first and the husband-slayer in the second poem are well realized and the emotional force the poems generate is due in part to the blighted quality of their speech. This was the poet's expressive intention, but her successes in the form are few in number, while the extreme irregularity of the lines cancels all poetic effect.

In the poems collected in *East Wind* the direction of advance was in the tightening of form. Nearly half of the thirteen poems are now written in meter. Moreover, "The Doll" is a further departure in that the woman who speaks the lines is a sophisticated artist instead of an unlettered country person. This *persona*, never used before, allowed the poet a new refinement and range of observation. The story she recounts is that of two old maids with a pathological attachment to a large French doll, and the tale of the two starved lives is controlled and filtered by the speaker's urbane wit.

"The Day That Was That Day," the second notable poem in *East Wind*, is an advance for another reason. Written in the shapeless verse of the earlier work, it is the story of a woman driven to suicide by the emotional poverty of her life. Like Hiram's widow and the husband-killer mentioned above, Minnie Green is one of Miss Lowell's few successes in realizing human character. The same pinched quality of speech used in the other poems contributes to our sense of her plight, but this is relieved here by three interludes of a highly poetic quality. At first glance it would seem that the poet is merely sketching in some decorative background for her tale, but this does not account for the deep resonance of the lines,

> *The wind rose, and the wind fell,*
> *And the day that was that day*
> *Floated under a high Heaven.*

"Home! Home! Home!"
Sang a robin in a spice-bush.
"Sun on a roof-tree! Sun on a roof-tree!"
Rang thin clouds
In a chord of silver across a placid sky. . . .

In their proper setting in the poem the three interludes are very striking. Their effect is to place these meager lives in a cosmic setting. In contrast to Minnie's choked life, Miss Lowell gives us the largeness and mystery of man's natural setting.

Ballads For Sale was the last of Miss Lowell's books to be published. This thick miscellany was well edited by Mrs. Russell, but the task she undertook was not solvable in any way that would do justice to Miss Lowell's gifts and the artistic stage she had reached at the end of her life. The poems consisted of the overflow from the poet's files, including many rejects from books she had published early in her career. Had Miss Lowell lived to fulfill her promise, it is likely that most of these poems would have been destroyed, but Mrs. Russell did not have that option.

Among these slight and brittle pieces there were a few poems of real substance, including some representing her most accomplished technique. One such poem is "Paradox," a lyric of extraordinary evocative power. Nothing else she wrote equals this poem in its ability to fuse a jewel-like hardness and brilliance with a compelling statement of her feelings about the would-be Beloved. Part of the beauty of expression consists in the gradual building of linked images of the Beloved and a fantastic jeweled garden so that a very complex structure of poetic associations emerges.

You are an amethyst to me,
Beating dark slabs of purple
Against quiet smoothnesses of heliotrope,
Sending the wine-color of torches
Rattling up against an avalanche of pale windy
   leaves. . . .

An amethyst garden you are to me,
And in your sands I write my poems,
And plant my heart for you in deathless yew-trees
That their leaves may shield you from the falling
    snow. . . .

                                              [*CP*, 555]

Other poems of interest in the book include a full and literal account of Amy's relationship with Mrs. Russell written for her "On Christmas Eve" as a gift, an elaborate love lyric, "Thorn Piece," the terse eroticism of "Carrefour," and a caustic self-portrait in "New Heavens For Old." In addition to these there is also the fine lyric, "On Looking at a Copy of Alice Meynell's Poems" which seems to belong among the poems of this kind collected in *What's O'Clock*. This last named volume, which won the Pulitzer Prize in 1926 and has been the most popular of her books as well, is the vindication of Miss Lowell's belief in the value of unhurried development and accumulation of powers. Its quality consists of a heightening of all that had gone before. It is not the journey completed but the sun at high noon after which there was to be the softened forms and golden light of afternoon.

                                III

                            Polyphonics

One of the reasons for her success was that Miss Lowell had found a means to do justice to her impressions and, at the same time, to integrate these with reflective, ratiocinative, and more purely emotive elements. That this was possible was due to her ten years of continual experimentation with novel forms of verse, which gained her a reputation as literary radical and filled her volumes with hundreds of pages of verbal exercises, all of which were needed to bring her designs to completion. But this does not mean that Miss Lowell ever devised one all-purpose formula for her work. It was not a question of a single method she consciously developed but rather of the possibility of composing in polyphonic sequence.

Already in her pre-Imagist period she was writing in the rhymed *vers libre* of the French, a mixed form seen at its best in "Patterns."[4] Somewhat later, in 1913 and 1914, she wrote extensively both in strict meters and in free verse of a high technical quality. Next came the quasi-epics in polyphonic prose, 1917-1918, with their requirement that she deal with a great variety of complex material within a single poem.[5] As she was successful in doing this, she gained skill in the control of unwieldy subject matter, and her composition gained a fluidity corresponding to these demands. All that remained was to use this suppleness to combine the various "voices"—her term for the different modes and devices of poetry—and one could have a poem which expanded and contracted, alternating between meter and free verse, as well as the many variations of these Miss Lowell herself had devised.

Quite often rhymed metrical verse was used as a point of departure for a delicate music which hovers above the banality of strict design as the rhythms stretch to fit each expressive purpose and rhyme-words fall expectedly like bell-notes. Examples of this technique can be found in "Texas," "Fool O' The Moon," "The Swans," and "Merely Statement." But this is one limited use of the form and its essential characteristic is its variability. One of the fullest uses of her technique can be found in the elegiac poem, "The Vow," inspired by a visit the poet made to Charleston, South Carolina in 1922 (*CP*, 451).

As Foster Damon has pointed out, Miss Lowell had lively feelings about the Civil War as the result of the animated family discussions of it she recalled from her childhood. In "The Vow" these memories combined with her taste for tropical richness and the sentiment which is best expressed in her line, "O loveliness of old, decaying haunted things" from another poem on Charleston's past. Moreover, Amy Lowell could identify with her subjects: the two proud ladies who sacrificed themselves by vowing never to leave their own garden until the South was free of Northern rule. The fact that both their ideals and their conduct were unrealistic merely added to the poignancy of the situation.

On the basis of these fused meanings and the impressions she gathered during her visit, Miss Lowell sets out to organize her far-ranging poem. The subject is the Pringle sisters and their useless defiance, but the note struck is that of human incompletion, a theme enlarged and dignified by association with the events of the Civil War:

> Tread softly, softly,
> Scuffle no dust.
> No common thoughts shall thrust
> Upon this peaceful decay,
> This mold and rust of yesterday.
> This is an altar with its incense blown away
> By the indifferent wind of a long, sad night;
> These are the precincts of the dead who die
> Unconquered. Haply
> You who haunt this place
> May deign some gesture of forgiveness
> To those of our sundered race
> Who come in all humility
> Asking an alms of pardon.
> Suffer us to feel an ease,
> A benefice of love poured down on us from these
>   magnolia-trees.
> That, when we leave you, we shall know the bitter
>   wound
> Of our long mutual scourging healed at last and
>   sound. . . .

The elegaic tone is sustained here in lines whose very appearance suggests the reticence of the emotions involved.

As she tells us, her words are directed by the need she feels for reconciliation of the "sundered race," and this has its verbal counterpart in the widely separated end-rhymes: softly, haply, humility, magnolia-trees—which drop down through the passage drawing it together with the most tenuous of bonds. In the last three lines quoted above there is a reference to love pouring down from the magnolias, and here the lines expand in summary of what has been said and in anticipation of the descriptive and narrative section that follows:

> Through an iron gate, fantastically scrolled and
>   garlanded,
> Along a path, green with moss, between two rows of
>   high magnolia-trees—
>   *How lightly the wind drips through the magnolias.*
>   *How slightly the magnolias bend to the wind.*
> It stands, pushed back into a corner of the piazza,
> A jouncing-board, with its paint scaled off,
> A jouncing-board which creaks when you sit upon it.
>   *The wind rattles the stiff leaves of the magnolias:*
>   *So may tinkling banjos drown the weeping of*
>   *women.*

The poem continues in this vein, giving us the story of the Pringle sisters detail by detail, and with the curious, abrupt interrruptions of thought seen above: *"How lightly the wind . . ."* which hold the poem to a high level of lyrical intensity. The vow having been made for so high a cause, the sisters play their chosen role to the end and leave their home and garden only in death. The beautiful conclusion of the poem is a variant of the opening, but its tone is more gathered, more firm, and more hurried. The poet reflects now that it is her obligation to find a moral in this gloomy story and press on with her other concerns.

I have given this account of the poem in order to show the diverse parts of which it is composed. In the opening passage Miss Lowell uses the rhymes and strongly marked stresses found in meter to concentrate and heighthen her emotional statement. But she has also used her freedom as a *vers-libriste* to bend and reorder the lines to match the shifting content of her thought. We find her doing this in the three long lines in the middle of this section. As her subject changes in the stanza that follows, so does her style, the lines exploding into energetic free verse as she turns to the tropical setting and the heroic acts and attitudes of the sisters. In this section the poet makes use of lyrical interjections in the style of her coruscating polyphonic prose developed some years earlier. Reduced in this way to short, disconnected passages and exploited for its brilliance, the high intensity form adds measurably to the poem's expressive effect. At the end of the long poem the verses are rounded by a return to the pattern of the opening, as noted above, but with the shift to a changed point of view as the result of the completed experience.

Part of the appeal of "The Vow" consists in a rhetorical excellence I have not described, but the purpose here is to illustrate the polyphonic sequence. Miss Lowell's most mature technical achievement, it is a real innovation which appears to be unique in English verse. By this means, the many "voices" of poetry—rhyme, meter, stanza, refrain, free verse, the intricate sound patterns of her polyphonic prose, and, finally, the use of key images or ideas which she called "return"—became fully available to catch the fleeting shapes of her thought. If this suggests clutter, it should be remembered that the technique consisted in the selection of those voices appropriate to the subject and that these are used in the polyphonic sequence required. There is also the element of spontaneity mentioned above. Had this technique been the result of a calculated plan, the freshness and charm inherent in it would have vanished.

One is led to this conclusion by a careful reading of polyphonic pieces such as "Purple Grackles" (*CP*, 447). Here the artistry consists in the alternation of descriptive passages of colloquial tone, like stanza one, with statements of a higher order of intensity and poetic form, as in stanza two. These components are drawn together by an effective

use of refrain, "The grackles have come," and in the conclusion there is a marked alteration in mood as the poet
ponders the meaning of seasonal change. What had been
a festive and humorous mixing between the poet-hostess
and a horde of kingly guests changes to a lesson in the
nature of things when they suddenly disappear. At this
point in the poem, the witty and loosely structured lines
contract and harden—become, in a word, the perfect expression of the sharpened awareness she now turns on the
scene about her. The section is introduced by a last use of
her refrain and a subtle intrusion of rhyme in "purple
head" and "flower beds," very widely separated, which
adds to the sense of finality in the passage:

> Come! Yes, they surely came.
> But they have gone.
> A moment ago the oak was full of them,
> They are not there now.
> Not a speck of a black wing,
> Not an eye-peep of a purple head.
> The grackles have gone,
> And I watch an Autumn storm
> Stripping the garden,
> Shouting black rain challenges
> To an old, limp summer
> Laid down to die in the flower-beds.

"Lilacs," also written at this time, is another New England poem of complex intentions (*CP*, 446). As we see
in the opening lines, it is more austere than "Purple
Grackles," the poet achieving the ultimate simplication
by reducing her statement to the naming of a series of distinct but somehow evocative colors. This passage is followed by other sharply focused images which are rendered
with an uncanny purity and freshness of line. So true are
all these pictures that the objects appear in a new light—
and what is usually taken as a miscellaneous catalogue
turns out to be the features of a "face." It is the face of

New England, and through the key symbolism of the lilac blooms Miss Lowell has elicited the spirit of a land and a people—

> You are brighter than apples,
> Sweeter than tulips,
> You are the great flood of our souls
> Bursting above the leaf-shapes of our hearts.

Somehow, the many bright images forming the body of this poem coalesce into a coherent design, and the division of the lines into three distinct movements makes possible the gradual rise to the assertion of a mystical identity between poet and country.

The merit of "Lilacs" consists in the discovery of oneness under the veil of diverse appearances, and it does this partly by the use of a unifying design. In "East, West, North, and South of a Man" the poet begins with a closely delimited theme, the four aspects of *a man*, and moves outward to diversity in a poem consisting of four loosely related movements (*CP*, 435). In fact, one may wonder if this is a single poem at all, or at least if this could be one man as the poet tells us in her title. But the purpose here is to dramatize her subject by the use of extreme instances presented in brilliant and contrasting images. Three of her portraits are in free verse but in the portrait of the itinerant peddler, the poet has used a jingling, broken-ended meter to suggest the inconsequence of the merchant's concerns. For the others, the warrior, the lover, and the scholar, she has used an expansive form of free verse and sumptuous settings to turn our thought in a transcendental direction. We can see this in the similes she uses in the opening lines of the poem, with their echo of the rhythm and refrain of the medieval ballad:

> He rides a white horse,
>   Mary Madonna,
> Dappled as clouds are dappled,
>   O Mary, Mary,
> And the leather of his harness is the colour of the sky.

Beginning with a knight seated on a horse, a practical man of action, we have next a reference to clouds and already in the fifth line of this poem, rhythm and image are intended to suggest infinite dimensions. Dimensions of this kind are also attributed to the handsome, gorgeously arrayed lover—"His voice is the sun in mid-heaven/Pouring on whirled ochre dahlias"—and in the climactic portrait of the scholar, said to be Miss Lowell herself, the poet sets before us the infinitude of the mind as the final measure of man:

> The walls of forbidden cities fall before him;
> He has but to tap a sheepskin to experience kingdoms,
> And circumstance drips from his fingers like dust. . . .
> He eats the centuries
> And lives a new life every twenty-four hours,
> So lengthening his own to an incalculable figure. . . .

The sense of magnitude we have in this poem is expressed in "The Green Parakeet" as well, but in the latter poem it is an ironic commentary on a story of tragic deprivation (*CP*, 467). On the one hand we see the world of nature with its startling beauty and freshness, symbolized by the parakeet as well as by talking and whimsical vines, trees, and barberry bushes. On the other, there is the mixed nature of man. As the poem begins, the protagonist ravishes a young, innocent girl. Although she does not resist and she conceives a love for him at once, the hero has deprived the girl of her purity, represented here by the death of the pet parakeet. Stricken by guilt, the lover first runs away to watch her from a distance.

> I stared at her from the farther side
> Of Hell, no space is great beside
> This space. I could not see her face
> Across such vastitude of space,
> And over it drowsed a darkened thing:
> A monster parakeet's green wing,
> The air was starred with parakeets.
> I turned and rushed into the streets. . . .

After a few days of covert observation of the deserted girl, some "odd obedience" in his feet compels him to rush out into the country. He then wears out his life moving restlessly from one place to another, "Bent double underneath the load/Of memory and second sight," while the specter of the bird haunts him. The story of guilty love is told in tight tetrameter couplets. Opening out from this are a number of polyphonic interludes developed along highly fanciful lines, whose effect is to interweave this tragedy with the life of natural things. At the conclusion of the poem the poet gives us a final image of the innocent creatures of nature set in contrast with the fevered state of man.

> The man scuffed across a bridge and up a steep hill. "Quietly, quietly," whispered the barberrybushes, and hid their scarlet tongues under their leaves. "Weep, Tree-Brothers," said the grapevines. But the long lines of trees only rustled and played hide and seek with the peeping moon. They were too tall to pay much heed to anything so small as an old man limping up a hill.

IV

Asepsis

Besides the impressions and combined forms we find in these polyphonic sequences, Amy Lowell was also writing many lyrics during the last years of her life. Some of these are among her best work of this type. The emotions are very fully developed and the content is matched by a corresponding richness of poetic invention. Perhaps the best single example would be "Song for a Viola D'Amore," already quoted in chapter one. Like many other lyrics she wrote at this time, the "Song" was inspired by Miss Lowell's feelings for her companion, but there is another and contrasting group even more expressive of the poet's inner history. These are the poems of asepsis: the bleeding of life by the denial of vital experience. The sense of tragic incompleteness, Miss Lowell's foremost theme, is presented with great emphasis in her poem, "New Heavens For Old."

I am useless.
What I do is nothing,
What I think has no savor.
There is an almanac between the windows:
It is of the year when I was born.

My fellows call me to join them. . . .
They are indecent and strut with the thought of it. . . .
Young men with naked hearts jeering between iron house-fronts,
Young men with naked bodies beneath their clothes
Passionately conscious of them,
Ready to strip off their clothes,
Ready to strip off their customs, their usual routine,
Clamoring for the rawness of life,
In love with appetite. . . .
They call for women and the women come,
They bare the whiteness of their lusts to the dead gaze of the old house-fronts,
They roar down the street like flame,
They explode upon the dead houses like new, sharp fire.
But I—
I arrange three roses in a Chinese vase. . . .
I fuss over their arrangement.
Then I sit in a South window. . . .
And think of Winter nights,
And field-mice crossing and re-crossing
The spot which will be my grave.

[*CP*, 574]

The poem is somewhat theatrical and over-drawn but it is interesting as a revelation of Miss Lowell's attitudes. Her description of the youth, "her fellows" who shout for her in this poem bearing "vermilion banners," defying the propriety represented by "the iron fronts of the houses" —this description is interesting in that it does not apply at all to her own time, but it is an accurate account of developments forty-five years after her death. There is an element of clairvoyance and even of prophecy here; but she does not tell us to what extent she sympathizes with the rebelliousness of her fellows. What is clear is that she places herself on the side of adventure and self-expression and equates excessive constraints with death.

The stiffling of the inner self is also her theme in the deeply meditated lyric, "On Looking at a Copy of Alice Meynell's Poems, Given Me Years Ago By A Friend" (*CP*, 536). This poem, treating Miss Lowell's loveless state, was inspired by news of the death of Alice Meynell and is addressed to Frances Dabney, a close friend who had died many years before. The history to which it refers concerns Miss Lowell's visit to Devonshire in 1899, in the company of Miss Dabney, when the future poet was suffering from a nervous breakdown. As stated above, the illness persisted through the remainder of Miss Lowell's youth, and in this poem she tells of the cause of the malady. It was not the English sea air which she required but a chance at life. For this reason Miss Dabney's gift of the book of poems was ironic. The theme of Miss Meynell's verse was the very experience through which Miss Lowell was passing, and reading the poems only sharpened her sense of loss:

> Silent the sea, the earth, the sky,
> And in my heart a silent weeping,
> Who has not sown can know no reaping
> Bitter conclusion and no lie. . . .

No future where there is no past!
O cherishing grief which laid me bare,
I wrapped you like a wintry air
About me. Poor enthusiast!

These are the unpromising ingredients the poet trans-
mutes into a preternatural radance. But it would be wrong
to assume that this is so because the feelings involved are
in some way pleasing to her or that her exaltation is due
to the stoic fortitude she expresses at the end of the poem.
Instead, we must look for the answer in another order of
experience she also traces in the poem. This reveals itself
in the hypnotic or hallucinatory quality of the images
with which she evokes the Devonshire sea-coast, the poetry
of Miss Meynell:

. . . like bronze cathedral bells
Down ancient lawns, or citadels
Thundering with gongs where choirs sang. . . .

and the act of remembrance itself that she compares to a
winking, spectral light. This experience of a deeper order
of existence cannot be described, except as she suggests it
in her images, but its importance lies in the fact that it
has invested and transformed the pain and deformity of
life with which this poem began.

The same process is at work in "Nuit Blanche," one of
the most accomplished of Amy Lowell's lyrics (*CP*, 474).
The French title means "white night" or sleeplessness, but
the meaning is modified if we reflect that Miss Lowell slept
during the day and worked in quiet and seclusion at night.
Taking these circumstances into account, the poem would
seem to express a total vacancy of life, the exhaustion of
normal interests and energies. However, the withdrawal of
feeling does not include indifference to sexual passion. And
we learn as well that it is not satiety that has inspired her
fatigue but a long-continued incompletion. Out of this
basic discord, the poet has fashioned a superb glissando,
sound and image being molded into a single seamless
whole.

I want no horns to rouse me up tonight,
And trumpets make too clamorous a ring
To fit my mood, it is so weary white
I have no wish for doing any thing.

A music coaxed from humming strings would please;
Not plucked, but drawn in creeping cadences
Across a sunset wall where some Marquise
Picks a pale rose amid strange silences.

The predominance of single syllable words here is imporant to her esthetic design. Along with the drawn-out pentameters, this slows the movement of her lines, the pronounced end-rhymes in alternate succession having the same retarding effect. The purpose is to suggest a slow awakening, and the mood set for this is symbolized by a continual stress on whiteness beginning with the title of the poem and ending with its last syllable. Nevertheless, her subject is not whiteness or nullity of life. Though this is the poet's mood, the scene to which she awakes is a romantic one, and we are aware from the first syllables that it is not an earthly ground.

This is expressed, first of all, by the sounds of music which recall the concerts Miss Lowell gave in her white and crystal library. In the poem, as it did in real life, the music stretches to enclose a garden, and here we have the heroine of "Patterns" again, now very subdued, but engaged in the same task of defining herself and the terms of her existence. It is sunset here, not the brilliant daylight of "Patterns," and there is no defiance at all. The brisk-paced sweep through a spring-time garden is replaced by lanquid movements whose meaning is focused in the pale rose the heroine picks "amid strange silences." If the rose symbolizes the bloodlessness of her life, the "strange silences" suggest her suffocated state, and in the third stanza this tragic figure dissolves completely into the twilight landscape:

> Ghostly and vaporous her gown sweeps by
> The twilight dusking wall. I hear her feet
> Delaying on the gravel, and a sigh,
> Briefly permitted, touches the air like sleet.

After this there is a transition to night and the poet herself reappears.

> And it is dark. I hear her feet no more.
> A red moon leers beyond the lily-tank,
> A drunken moon, ogling a sycamore,
> Running long fingers down its shining flank.

> A lurching moon, as nimble as a clown,
> Cuddling the flowers and trees which burn like glass.
> Red, kissing lips I feel you on my gown—
> Kiss me, red lips, and then pass—pass.

> Music, you are pitiless tonight,
> And I so old, so cold, so languorously white.

At first sight it seems that there has been a falling away from the elevation of the first three stanzas. Here we have the moon as clown in lustful relation with the objects of the garden. But then we notice the artistry that moves the poem first from humming strings to the faded marquise and finally embraces a sharply contrasting scene. The subject now is the pain of bondage to the flesh. This is vividly expressed in the most poignant passage in the poem: "Red, kissing lips I feel you on my gown—/Kiss me, red lips, and then pass—pass." At this point there is a sudden break in the form and tone of the poem, which is the verbal equivalent of the snapping of her mood. No longer equal to the spirituality of the music and the harmonies of the moonlit scene, there is a collapse to awareness of the discords of her life.

"Nuit Blanche" and "Alice Meynell" can be seen in this

way as admixtures of tragic incompletion and the glimpsing of transcendent design. In "Folie de Minuit," on the other hand, we have a direct challenge to the flawed state in which man finds himself. In the poem she wrote to a pious friend many years earlier ("To Elizabeth Ward Perkins"), Miss Lowell had stood uneasily outside a church door incapable of the surrender of her viewpoint for the sake of the comfort inside. In "Folie de Minuit," she enters a cathedral as an invader with the purpose of summoning God with an offering of music which she is still playing, now hopelessly, at the end of the poem (*CP*, 471).

As the poem implies, man not only suffers personal unfulfillment, but as sentient and rational being, he suffers also because of the withdrawal of the fatherhood of his Creator. Unique and isolated in the natural scheme of things, man can only complete his own selfhood in converse with the *corresponding* Power he expresses. To speak in monologue is unsatisfying. Only the responses of an equal can tell us of ourselves. "Folie de Minuit" was a reaction, in part, to an earnest rereading of the Bible Miss Lowell undertook at this time. In her conception, the god-man Christ bears unmistakable signs of divinity. But Jesus lived long ago and since the passing of that era God has been noticeably quiescent. At least, this was Miss Lowell's view and the cathedral we enter in her poem is a cold and untenanted religious museum.

The quality of her emotion is given at once in a fervid opening passage where trochaic accents, emphatic rhymes (word-lord, city-pity, cold-boldest), and the insistence on o and or combinations, as in snow and lord, all contribute to the intensity of effect:

> No word, no word, O Lord God!
> Hanging above the shivering pillars
> Like thunder over a brazen city.

Pity, is there pity?
Does pity pour from the multiform points
Of snow crystals?
If the throats of the organ pipes
Are numb with cold,
Can the boldest bellows' blast
Melt their now dumb hosannas?

We notice first the explosive energy which seems to topple or transform the holy precincts around the poet. Part of this establishment or religious machinery is the idea of the loving God, but the Deity which is conceived here is a remote and terrifying power like "thunder over a brazen city." In contrast, man has a need for pity—not because he is weak but because he is in darkness. This darkness hangs over the whole poem, filling the cathedral and acting as the backdrop to the theatrical "midnight burials" of stanza four. In this context, the poet asks how man can expect pity in a universe symbolized by the icy perfection of the snowflake. Such hopes are illusory, it seems, but these same "multiform points," obviously the product of intelligence, show that the universe is "haunted."

Since this is her conviction, a possibility that remains is to dwell on those precincts and those passages of history where the Divine was manifest in another form. This would seem to be true of ancient Palestine and the European "age of faith" which furnish the content for the section which follows, including its effulgent image of Christ:

No word, august and brooding God!
No shriveled spectre of an aching tone
Can pierce those banners
Which hide your face, your hands,
Your feet at whose slight tread
Frore water curds to freckled sands
Seaweed encrusted. . . .

In this passage the use of s sounds which unify the section as a whole, the use of the dental sounds d and t in the last three lines, and the unexpected rhyme in sands-hands add to the tightness of design. Following on this, the poet says that she had hoped to break the silence of the church with golden anthems of the kind sung by the victorious Hebrews.

Though this was her purpose, everything she sees in the cathedral is choked with silence and dust, and this has affected her as well. In an extraordinary image, "My finger-tips are cast in a shard of silence," she gives us her sense of the spiritual impotence of man. Without an answer from the God of the shadows, there is no possibility of communion or means by which man may truly define himself. This is the cause for the despair of the poem:

> Pity me, then,
> Who cry with wingless psalms,
> Spellbound in midnight and chill organ pipes. . . .

But it is also important to note that none of these considerations deters the poet, who is still playing religious anthems at the end of the poem.

V

Transcendence

The failure of the spiritual quest that Miss Lowell describes in "Folie de Minuit" must be qualified by reference to the mystical order of experience we have traced in her poetry. Mystic awareness is the implied subject of many poems in *What's O'Clock* and it is the predominate note of the volume. First of all, it is at the center of her long, blank-verse narrative, "Which Being Interpreted Is As May Be or Otherwise," whose setting is the belfry

of a cathedral and whose story is a symbolic contest be-
ween earth forces, represented by the statue of a satanic
king, and the forces of spiritual aspiration, represented
by the frail and other-worldly scholar, Neron (*CP*, 453). In
the vividly imagined "In Excelsis," remarkable for its
ability to sustain the note of rapture or ecstasy, adoration
of the beloved one becomes fused with religious emotion.
And "Evelyn Ray," a narrative lyric, interweaves a stark
human tragedy with one of the poet's most evocative
numinous landscapes.

This same dual theme is found in the six sonnets written
for "Eleonora Duse," that may be considered a conscious
summation of the thought and experience of the poet
(*CP*, 479). The occasion that inspired them favored this
purpose. The poems were composed in December, 1923, at
the height of her powers and in her last recorded "burst"
of poetic creativity. Because of her circumstances at this
moment and the circumstances of Duse, it was natural that
the poet would be led to a special view of life and the place
of the artist. However, the reader of these sonnets should
not be misled into seeing them as a romanticizing of the
lives and attitudes described. The strangeness of the poem
is not due to sentimental distortion but rather to its fidel-
ity to the nature of the two women involved. For this reason, we are obliged to accept these revelations in the
character and form which Miss Lowell gave them.

The history began in the Boston theater in 1902 when
a performance by Duse stirred new life in the neuras-
thenic, twenty-eight year old Miss Lowell. In terms of
tragic deprivations there were similarities in the lives of
the two women. We know from Miss Lowell's earliest
poem that she saw in Duse the mastery and transcendence
of this experience. That it could produce an awareness
that would serve the purposes of art was a second discovery for her. For this reason it was Duse—with her uncanny power to detect and transmit the spiritual vibration—
and not a poet of impressive formal achievement who always remained Miss Lowell's artistic ideal.

Nevertheless, Miss Lowell was unable to see Duse from 1902 to 1923 and when she encountered her again both of them were drawing to the close of their lives. Though these facts do not appear in her poem, Duse at this time was broken by age and ill health and accepted the hardships of an American tour only to gain funds for an art theater she hoped to establish in Italy. In view of these handicaps, the emaciated and white-haired actress must have made a remarkable effort. The tour calling for her appearance even as a young woman, became a succession of triumphs. Near the close of her New York engagement, Amy saw her in two performances, and then again on December 4 and 6 in Boston. The two had exchanged letters and after the second of the Boston appearances Duse came to spend a day at Sevenels. The day-long visit was a success, and that encounter, plus other performances Miss Lowell was able to see before the sudden death of the actress a few months later, furnished the inspiration for her poem:

> Seeing's believing, so the ancient word
> Chills buds to shrivelled powder flecks, turns flax
> To smoky heaps of straw whose small flames wax
> Only to gasp and die. The thing's absurd!
> Have blind men ever seen or deaf men heard?
> What one beholds but measures what one lacks.
> Where is the prism to draw gold from blacks,
> Or flash the iris colors of a bird?
> Not in the eye, be sure, nor in the ear,
> Nor in an instrument of twisted glass,
> Yet there are sights I see and sounds I hear
> Which ripple me like water as they pass.
> This that I give you for a dear love's sake
> Is curling noise of waves marching along a lake.

The dematerialization of vision, an important element in this poem, is supported by a sound-patterning which stresses high, light sounds (chills, shrivelled, iris, eye, twisted, blind, etc.) as well as a pattern of images which suggest an airy dryness: "Chills buds to shrivelled powder flecks." Emerging from this is the affirmation of the mystical insight on which Duse's power is based. Through this gift we become aware of the incompleteness of the phenomenal world which is shown to depend on essences of which we have no direct sensory awareness. In spite of its limitations, the world of sense participates in the transcendent design and is capable of stirring profound emotions: "Yet there are sights I see. . . ." After this amendment of her thesis, the poet concludes the sonnet by saying that she is writing these poems to express her love for Duse.

In sonnet two we are told of the poem's character as a letter to her friend; and there is a second challenge to the empiricist who would confine the world to what we can see:

> Seeing's believing? What then would you see?
> A chamfered dragon? Three spear-heads of steel?
> A motto done in flowered charactry?
> The thin outline of Mercury's winged heel?
> Look closer, do you see a name, a face,
> Or just a cloud dropped down before a holy place?

The images have the crisp, linear quality we found in sonnet one and we find again in lines six and seven with their account of the decisive effect of Duse on her life: "Like melted ice/I took the form and froze so" . . . Given the facts of their encounter, we are able to accept the note of worship in the last line as well as the reverence she expresses in sonnet three:

> Lady, to whose enchantment I took shape
> So long ago, though carven to your grace,
> Bearing, like quickened wood, your sweet sad face
> Cut in my flesh, yet may I not escape
> My limitations: words that jibe and gape
> After your loveliness and make grimace
> And travesty where they should interlace
> The weave of sun-spun ocean round a cape. . . .

Eloquent as these lines are, they are a *diminuendo* from the
fever of the two preceding sonnets in which the poet affirms
her transcendental vision. The headlong rush there is replaced by a slow, curved movement as the poet goes on to
describe the meaning of Duse for her life and what Duse is
in herself. For this purpose abstract or conceptual language
is inadequate, so she turns to nature to suggest the qualities
of the artist, concluding with a statement of Duse's affect
on her world: "All that you are mingles as one sole cry/To
point a world aright which is so much awry."

These lines anticipate the theme Miss Lowell develops
in the two sonnets that follow. The first of these, number
four, emphasizes the special character of Duse's art. So great
is the understanding of this artist that it seems to embrace
the whole experience of mankind. Because of her awareness
of human nature and its needs, Duse acts as a moral force
which calls men to their higher selves, being picked, the
poet says:

> . . . to pierce, reveal, and soothe again.
> Shattering by means of you the tinsel creeds
> Offered as meat to the pinched hearts of man.
> So, sacrificing you, she fed those others
> Who bless you in their prayers even before their
>   mothers.

The somewhat flattened tone of the last line calls attention to a peculiarity of her form. In all six sonnets the last
line is drawn out by an extra two or four syllables like a
whip snapped at the end, breaking the symmetry for a moment and propelling the reader to the next sonnet. It is
likely that the device originated by accident when the poet
found she had twelve syllables, an alexandrine, at the end
of sonnet one. But from that point forward its use is deliberate, and it achieves her purpose in giving added weight
to the final statement.

Sonnet five extends and varies the treatment of the theme

introduced in three, but there is a new inrush of feeling as
the poet turns to consider Duse in the character now of prophetess.

> Life seized you with her iron hands and shook
> The fire of your boundless burning out
> To fall on us, poor little ragged rout
> Of common men, till like a flaming book
> We, letters of a message, flashed and took
> The fiery flare of prophecy, devout
> Tourches to bear your oil, a dazzling shout,
> The liquid golden running of a brook.
> Who, being upborne on racing streams of light,
> Seeing new heavens sprung from dusty hells,
> Considered you, and what might be your plight,
> Robbed, plundered—since Life's cruel plan compels
> The perfect sacrifice of one great soul
> To make a myriad others even a whit more whole.

This is the most declamatory of the six sonnets, if that
word can be taken in a favorable sense, the purpose of the
poet being to proclaim the transcendent stature of Duse.
The sense of urgency which fills her mind is expressed in
the strongly marked accents and rhymes ("Robbed, plun-
dered"—"Life seized you"; shook - book - brook etc.), but
it comes as well from the meaning of her statements. There
is an urgent need to affirm, for the experience involved
turns on a tragic opposition. As men are drawn up by the
fire of the prophetess and her revelation of a divine message, so they become her "torches" and finally are "upborne
on racing streams of light"—this same process of spiri-
tualization exacts unfulfillment and exhaustion for Duse,
a tragedy which the poet generalizes as a law of the race
in the concluding three lines of the poem.

This being true, Duse is both victor and vanquished as
we reach the last section of the poem. But sonnet six, very
likely the peak of Miss Lowell's art, is informed by a profundity of vision which transforms once more our view

of Duse and permits the poet to conclude her poem on a
note of somber exaltation:

> Seeing you stand once more before my eyes
> In your pale dignity and tenderness,
> Wearing your frailty like a misty dress
> Draped over the great glamor which denies
> To years their domination, all disguise
> Time can achieve is but to add a stress,
> A finer finess, as though some caress
> Touched you a moment to a strange surprise.
> Seeing you after these long lengths of years
> I only know the glory come again,
> A majesty bewildered by my tears,
> A golden sun spangling slant shafts of rain,
> Moonlight delaying by a sick man's bed,
> A rush of daffodils where wastes of dried leaves
>   spread.

Taking account of this sonnet as a whole, we notice first
the perfect correspondence between idea and form. Since
her purpose is to express a rarefied state of mind, she has
given her lines the same delicate tonality that we found in
sonnet one. This is emphasized by the lightness and the
chiming of the sounds—dignity, frailty, and misty all
falling together in a sequence of two lines—as well as the
graceful pauses in rhythm which follow the final word of
nearly every line. The image which this sonnet evokes is
that of the beauty of Duse as she appeared before her
audiences in 1923, audiences which were often discomfited
by her thinness and pallor but stayed on to be caught in the
web woven by her hands and the rapt perfection of her
movements. As always, she had refused to wear makeup on
this last tour. "I make myself up morally," she said, and did
nothing to disguise her white hair.

It is essential to know these facts in order to do justice
to the poet's conception. Duse, never possessed of physical
allure, was now the shell of her former self. But it does not

follow from this that the poet was deceived or deceiving. Rather, this *was* her meaning in a deeper sense. The beauty that she saw in Duse was not in the flesh at all, and the passage of years had only accentuated it. *This* is the "great glamour" which enchanted her, which can annul time, and which she hastens to conjoin with those superb images of renewal and healing in the concluding lines of the poem. In doing this she crystalizes the main theme of her poetry: divinity is one whteher glimpsed in a sunset, a landscape, or a human face. But this perception is not new to poetry. What is unique here is the evidence of her experience. If we look back now to the glowing images of this poem and ponder what she tells us there about her response to Duse, we can only conclude that she was participating in an exalted spiritual reality and this ecstasy is the record she left of it in her poetry.

Notes

CHAPTER ONE

1. Entry for Jan. 23, 1889, unpublished diaries of Amy Lowell, Houghton Library manuscript at Harvard. The statements which follow refer to the whole content and tone of these diaries.

2. *The Complete Poetical Works of Amy Lowell* (Boston, 1955), p. 18. Subsequent references to page numbers in this volume will appear in the text after the abbreviation, *CP*.

3. This photograph has been reproduced in Robert Phelps and Peter Deane, *A Scrapbook Almanac of the Anglo-American Literary Scene* (New York, 1968). Louis Untermeyer describes it in his volume of memoirs, *From Another World*, pp. 119-20.

4. The writings concerned are reviews of the poet's three posthumous volumes published in *Poetry* (Dec. 1925), XXVII, 154-58; (Dec. 1926), XXIX, 160-63; and (Mar. 1928), 338-43.

5. *Saturday Review* (May 30, 1925), I, 787.

6. S. Folster Damon, *Amy Lowell*, (Boston, 1935), pp. 525-51. Subsequent references to page numbers in this biography will appear in the text after the author's name in parenthesis.

7. Feb. 21, 1925, I, 550.

8. Winfield T. Scott, *Exiles and Fabrications* (New York, 1961), p. 114.

9. Horace Gregory, *Amy Lowell* (New York, 1958), pp. 37-38.

10. Louis Untermeyer, *From Another World*, (New York, 1939), p. 119.

11. Louis Untermeyer, editor, *The Letters of Robert Frost to Louis Untermeyer* (New York, 1963), pp. 148-49.

12. See Elizabeth Ward Perkins, "Amy Lowell of New England," *Scribners*, LXXXII, 330-31, and L. Untermeyer, *op. cit.*, pp. 100-101.

13. The essay is from *The Cafe Royal and Other Essays* (London, 1923), and is quoted by Gregory, *op. cit.*, pp. 38-9.

14. Bertita Harding, *Age Cannot Wither* (Philadelphia, 1947), p. 116.

15. *Op. cit.*, p. 330.

16. John Livingston Lowes, *Essays in Appreciation* (Boston, 1936), p. 168.

17. In his book on *Poetic Process* (London, 1953), pp. xxxiii-xxxiv, George Whalley discusses Goethe's view of the "double nature" of the artist, concluding that "Androgynous the great artist certainly is, but in respect to consciousness and not of creativity."

18. Jean Star Untermeyer takes up this point in her memoirs *Private Collection* (New York, 1965), p. 283, *a propos* of the commanding wife of the sculptor, Gaston Lachaise, and then names Cosima Wagner, Alma Mahler (also married to Franz Werfel and Walter Gropius), and Frieda

Lawrence in this same category. Most war-like and irrespressible of all was Pauline de Ahma, wife of Richard Strauss, whose fantastic behavior is described by Barbara Tuchman in *The Proud Tower* (New York, 1965) pp. 308-11.

19. The phrase is that of Damon, p. 14, who includes a history of the Lowells in Chapter Two of his biography.

20. *Op. cit.*, p. 329.

21. Diary entry, Nov. 24, 1889.

CHAPTER TWO

1. The building in question is the main public library in Toledo, Ohio, constructed in 1939.

2. See Amy Lowell, "Sevenels," *Touchstone*, VII (June, 1920), 210-18; reprinted in H. F. MacNair, editor, *Florence Ayscough and Amy Lowell* (Chicago, 1945), p. 250.

3. The quotation is from a description of the library by Elizabeth Sergeant, *Fire Under The Andes* (New York, 1927), p. 14.

4. Stars, sun, and moon used symbolically make up an important feature of this first volume.

5. This is from "Eleonora Duse," her first poem written as an adult. It is reprinted in *CP*. p. 593.

6. In *A Dome* beauty is not an absolute but a symbol of the Divine. In the preface to *Tendencies in Modern American Poetry* (New York, 1971), p. vii, Amy Lowell writes that the world has gained so much intrinsic value and importance for the modern poets "That they have no need to dwell constantly on its symbolic meaning." The point to note is that she regarded the world that is manifest to our senses as the expression of another reality: "The pledge of greater majesty unseen" she says of a mountain in "Monadnock in Early Spring," *CP*. p. 15.

7. The poem is reprinted on page nine of the collected edition. The title which is in Greek means "thirst".

CHAPTER THREE

Besides the five books of original verse published during these years, there were two critical studies of modern French and American poets, three Imagist anthologies supervised by Miss Lowell, and *Phantasms of War*, eleven long war poems, which has never issued. A complete listing of the essays appears in a bibliography printed at the end of Damon's biography of Miss Lowell.

2. This book was republished in London in 1965 as part of a collection called *A Lume Spento and Other Early Poems.* The preface appears on page 87 in this edition.

3. *Collected Poems,* 1940, pp. 22-23

4. Reprinted in *Modern American Poetry,* Louis Untermeyer, editor (New York, 1950), pp. 332-35.

5. A short history of this phase of Imagism is given by William Pratt in *The Imagist Poem* (New York, 1963), pp. 14-16.

6. The most important of these is his article in *Poetry,* I, 200-206, "A Few Don'ts By An Imagist," which appeared in March, 1913, just as he was launching the new Imagist movement.

7. *Collected Poems* (New York, 1940), p. 82.

8. Earl Miner, *The Japanese Tradition in British and American Literature* (Princeton, 1966), pp. 68-69.

9. William Barrett, editor of *Zen Buddhism: Selected Writings of D. T. Suzuki* (New York, 1956), discusses the significance of Oriental thought for the West in his introduction, pp. vii-xiv.

10. Alan W. Watts, *The Way of Zen* (New York, 1957), preface, pp. ix-x. Subsequent references to this book will be included in the text in parentheses.

11. Edna B. Stephens, *John Gould Fletcher* (New York, 1967), p. 55.

12. Quoted in Herbert Read, *Icon and Idea* (New York, 1965), p. 118.

13. Huston Smith, *The Religions of Man* (New York, 1958), p. 143.

14. *Ibid.*

15. Smith, p. 134.

16. *The English Novel* (New York, 1953), pp. 153-54.

17. See William Van O'Connor, *The Shaping Spirit: A Study of Wallace Stevens* (Chicago, 1950), pp. 26-63.

18. *The Social History of Art,* Vol. IV (New York 1967), pp. 166-225.

19. *Rococo to Cubism in Art and Literature* (New York, 1960), p. 171.

20. *Op cit.,* pp. 183-84 and pp. 178-79.

21. Francois Mathey, *The Impressionists* (New York, 1967) p. 200

22. Sypher, p. 181.

23. Sir Herbert Read, *The True Voice of Feeling* (New York, 1953), 103.

24. Read, pp. 108-9.

25. This is not stated in the passage but it is implied, and it is the sense of his theory as a whole. William Pratt, p. 28, quotes Hulme as saying: "Images in verse are not mere decoration, but the very essence of an intuitive language."

26. See Hynes, editor, *Further Speculations of T. E. Hulme,* (Minneapolis, 1955), p. 72.

27. Hynes, pp. 67-76.

28. Published in Hynes, p. 82.

29. Miner, p. 100.

30. Reprinted by Pratt, p. 41.

31. This point is made by Smith, pp. 137-38.

32. At the end of 1914, John Gould Fletcher returned to the United States and settled in Boston for two years' time. There followed a period of close intellectual collaboration between Fletcher and Miss Lowell, the two of them seeing each other several times a week. Fletcher has stated that at this time Zen Buddhist principles were upper-most in his mind. See the preface to his book, *Japanese Prints* (Boston, 1918). Fletcher had also been deeply affected by French Impressionist painting during his residence in Europe.

Chapter Four

1. "Sumptuous Destitution" included in *Emily Dickinson: A Collection of Critical Essays*, Richard B. Sewall, editor (Englewood Cliffs, 1963), p. 134.

2. Horace Gregory, *A History of American Poetry: 1900-1940* (New York, 1942), p. 188. Gregory gives a much more appreciative picture of Amy Lowell here than he does in his full-length study of her published sixteen years later when she had sunk into obscurity.

3. "Nationalism in Art," Poetry, V (Oct., 1914), 37.

4. *A History of American Poetry*, p. 339.

5. See Philip L. Gerber, *Robert Frost*, (New York, 1967).

6. See his book, *Form and Style in Poetry* (London, 1928), p. 100.

7. Quoted by Herbert Read in *Icon and Ideas*, p. 120.

8. Read, *The True Voice*, p. 107.

Chapter Five

1. *John Keats*, I, pp. 531-32.

2. Quoted by Harley F. MacNair, p. 277.

3. The photo is reprinted by Ferris Greenslet, *The Lowells and Their Seven Worlds* (Boston, 1946), p. 389.

4. "Before The Altar," *CP*, p. 1, which was quoted in chapter two, was written in 1912 before Miss Lowell had heard of the Imagists. It was the result of her discovery of French free verse, according to Damon, p. 185.

5. See *Can Grande's Castle, CP*, pp. 153-201.

Selective Bibliography

I. THE WRITINGS OF AMY LOWELL
The correspondence and private papers of Amy Lowell are in the manuscript collection of the Houghton Library, Harvard University. The original copies of her letters to Harriet Monroe, 1912-1924, may be found in the manuscript collection of the University of Chicago. A list of the letters, articles and reviews which Miss Lowell contributed to periodicals is included in a supplement to the biography by S. Foster Damon.

1. Collections
The Complete Poetical Works. Boston: Houghton Mifflin, 1955.
Poetry and Poets. Boston: Houghton Mifflin, 1930. This is a collection of some of her more important critical writings.
Lowes, John Livingston, editor. *Selected Poems of Amy Lowell.* Boston: Houghton Mifflin, 1928.
MacNair, Harley F., editor. *Florence Ayscough and Amy Lowell: Correspondence of a Friendship.* Chicago: University of Chicago Press, 1945.
Ruihley, G. R., editor. *A Shard of Silence: Selected Poems of Amy Lowell.* New York: Twayne, 1957.
Seymour, Peter, Editor. *The Touch of You: Poems of Love and Beauty by Amy Lowell.* Kansas City: Hallmark, 1972.

2. Individual Works
A Dome of Many-Coloured Glass. Boston: Houghton Mifflin, 1912.
Sword Blades and Poppy Seed. New York: Macmillan, 1914.
Six French Poets. New York: Macmillan, 1915.
Men, Women, and Ghosts. New York: Macmillan, 1916.
Tendencies in Modern American Poetry. New York: Macmillan, 1917.
Can Grande's Castle. New York: Macmillan, 1918.
Pictures of the Floating World. New York: Macmillan, 1919.
Legends. Boston: Houghton Mifflin, 1921.
Fir-Flower Tablets. (in collaboration with Florence Ayscough). Boston: Houghton Mifflin, 1921.

A Critical Fable. Boston: Houghton Mifflin, 1922. Reprinted
   1973, R. West, editor.
John Keats. Boston: Houghton Mifflin, 1925. Reprinted 1969,
   Archon Books.
What's O'Clock. Boston: Houghton Mifflin, 1925.
East Wind. Boston: Houghton Mifflin, 1926.
Ballads For Sale. Boston: Houghton Mifflin, 1927.

3. Bibliographies
In the *Bulletin of Bibliography*, XV (1933-34), 8-9, 25-6, 50-3,
   Frances Kemp includes an annotated list of the books and
   essays of Amy Lowell as well as writings about her.
The first printing of all her published writings is listed by S.
   Foster Damon in his biography, *Amy Lowell.* In *Articles on
   American Literature: 1900-1950*, Lewis Leary lists fifty-nine
   essays on Amy Lowell of many varieties and shades of opinion.

II. STUDIES OF MISS LOWELL AND HER WORK

Books
Wood, Clement. *Amy Lowell.* New York: Harold Vinal, 1926.
   This is not in any sense a serious study but a statement of the
   author's violent dislike for Amy Lowell and her work.
Damon, S. Foster. *Amy Lowell.* Boston: Houghton Mifflin, 1935.
   This is a very carefully prepared account of Miss Lowell's
   entire life and work including generous portions of her
   correspondence.
Gregory, Horace. *Amy Lowell.* New York: Thomas Nelson, 1958.
   The author has a marked antipathy for Amy Lowell and her
   poetry and expresses it in this volume. Except for his discussion of *John Keats*, his conclusions here are highly suspect.

2 Articles and Parts of Books.
   (Only essays of special interest are listed here).
Cestre, Carl. "L'Oeuvre Poetique d'Amy Lowell," *Revue Anglo-
   Americaine*, II (Aug. 1925), 481-500. Cestre appears somewhat
   confused about the nature of Amy Lowell's poetry but he writes
   about its spirituality with beauty and distinction.

Heiney, Donald. *Recent American Literature*. New York: Barron's, 1958, pp. 461-67. A brief overview of Amy Lowell which affirms her value and attacks the standard criticism of her poetry.

Kizer, Helen Bullis. "Amy Lowell: A Personality." *North American Review*, CCVII (May, 1918), 736-47. Contains important insights but they are not elaborated.

Perkins, Elizabeth Ward, "Amy Lowell of New England," *Scribners*, LXXXII (1926), 330-34. An account of the poet as she appeared to a close friend at various stages of her life. This is one of the most informative essays on her.

Sergeant, Elizabeth S. *Fire Under The Andes*. New York: Alfred A. Knopf, 1927, pp. 11-32. The habits, personality, and home of the poet very eloquently described by a long-time friend.

Tupper, James W. "The Poetry of Amy Lowell," *Sewanee Review*, XXVIII (Jan. 1920), 37-53. A substantial study written from a sympathetic point of view.

Untermeyer, Jean Starr. *Private Collection*. New York: Alfred A. Knopf, 1965, pp. 74-89. Personal memories of Amy Lowell which emphasize her courage.

Untermeyer, Louis. *From Another World*. New York: Harcourt Brace, 1939, pp. 99-125. The Amy Lowell of legend described in vivid language.

Widdemer, Margaret. *Golden Friends I Had*. New York: Doubleday, 1964, pp. 107-22. Recollections of the poet and observations on her personality.

Chronology

1874   Born February 9 at Brookline, Massachusetts, fifth child of Augustus and Katherine Lawrence, tenth generation of senior line of Lowell family.

1880-1891 Educated by governesses and in private schools until age of seventeen.

1882   Travels in Europe with parents and suffers nervous disorder as result of over-rapid pace.

1883   Travels across the U. S. to California; first appearance of obesity resulting from glandular disturbance; brother Percival begins ten years' residence in Japan stirring Amy's life-long interest in the Orient.

1888   Marriage of sister, Bessie, leaves Amy alone with aging parents.

1891   Schooling ends; makes debut in Boston society.

1895   Death of Amy's mother; Percival, now an astronomer, begins to publish advanced scientific views.

1896-1897 Travels in southern Europe and on a river-boat in Egypt.

1898   Effort to lose weight by diet and travel fails; at home suffers prolonged nervous breakdown.

1898-1899 Lives in California and in Devonshire, England, as an invalid.

1900   Augustus dies; Amy inherits Sevenels, the family estate, and substantial fortune; takes up minor civic duties for schools and libraries.

1902   Aged twenty-eight, sees Duse on stage and is moved to become poet; begins ten years' study and apprenticeship as a poet.

1905   Spends summer in Europe attended by a nurse.

1908   Visits France, Italy, Greece, and Turkey with a party of friends.

1909   Takes part in private theatricals as actress and director; brother Abbott Lawrence becomes president of Harvard.

1910   First poem, "A Fixed Idea" appears in print in *Atlantic Monthly.*

1912   Meets Ada Russell, her companion from 1914-1925; first book, *A Dome of Many-Coloured Glass*, is published and fails.

1913   Travels to England to study Imagism with Pound, H. D., and Fletcher; begins to write poems in her characteristic pictorial style.

1914   Returns to England and becomes leader of the Imagists; publishes *Sword Blades and Poppy Seed*, written in a controversial free verse style.

1915-1918   Period of poetic renaissance in U. S.; through countless lectures, readings, essays, and her own poems takes leadership of the movement; publishes *Six French Poets*, 1915, *Men, Women, and Ghosts*, 1916, *Tendencies in Modern American Poetry*, 1917, and *Can Grande's Castle*, 1918, the latter in a novel prose poetry.

1916   Injures herself in carriage accident causing umbilical hernia after suffering second accident in 1918.

1919   *Pictures of the Floating World*, poems reflecting her study of the Orient, becomes a best-seller.

1918-1921   Four operations for hernia are unsuccessful; the effects of this and overwork seriously undermine her health.

1921   Publishes *Legends* in May; in December, publishes *Fir Flower Tablets*, translations from the Chinese.

1922   *A Critical Fable*, off-hand, humorous comments on fellow poets; begins work on two volume study of Keats.

1923   Travels to New Jersey, New York, Ohio, Indiana, Illinois, Wisconsin, Minnesota, Nebraska, and Ontario, Canada in last extended lecture tour, January 30 to March 10.

1925   *John Keats* published in February; suffers physical collapse on April 10; dies on May 12; *What's O'Clock* is published and wins Pulitzer Prize.

1926-1930 Posthumous collections: *East Wind*, 1926; *Ballads For Sale*, 1927; *Selected Poems*, 1928, edited by J. L. Lowes; *Poetry and Poets*, selected criticism, 1930.

1955 *The Complete Poetical Works of Amy Lowell.*

1957 *A Shard of Silence, Selected Poems*, edited by G. R. Ruihley.

Index